KU-692-937

Aspects of modern sociology

The social structure of modern Britain

GENERAL EDITORS

John Barron Mays
Eleanor Rathbone Professor of Sociology, University of Liverpool

Maurice Craft
Senior Lecturer in Education, University of Exeter

Rural Life
Patterns and Processes

Gwyn E. Jones, B.A., B.Litt.

Lecturer in Rural Sociology,
Agricultural Extension and Rural Development Centre,
University of Reading.

Longman

LONGMAN GROUP LIMITED
London

Associated companies, branches and representatives throughout the world

© *Longman Group Limited 1973*

First published 1973

ISBN 0 582 48006 X Cased
0 582 48007 8 Paper

Printed in Hong Kong by
The Continental Printing Co Ltd

Contents

Editors' Preface

British higher education is now witnessing a very rapid expansion of teaching and research in the social sciences, and, in particular, in sociology. This new series has been designed for courses offered by universities, colleges of education, colleges of technology, and colleges of further education to meet the needs of students training for social work, teaching and a wide variety of other professions. It does not attempt a comprehensive treatment of the whole field of sociology, but concentrates on the social structure of modern Britain which forms a central feature of most university and college sociology courses in this country. Its purpose is to offer an analysis of our contemporary society through the study of basic demographic, ideological and structural features, and through the study of such major social institutions as the family, education, the economic and political structure, and so on.

The aim has been to produce a series of introductory texts which will in combination form the basis for a sustained course of study, but each volume has been designed as a single whole and can be read in its own right.

We hope that the topics covered in the series will prove attractive to a wide reading public and that, in addition to students, others who wish to know more than is readily available about the nature and structure of their own society will find them of interest.

JOHN BARRON MAYS
MAURICE CRAFT

Acknowledgements

We are grateful to the following for permission to reproduce copyright material:
The Controller of Her Majesty's Stationery Office for four tables based on data from *Agricultural Statistics* and various *Population Census Volumes* and also two tables based on statistics from Royal Commission on Local Government in England, *Research Studies 9 – Community Attitudes Survey: England,* The Macmillan Company for one table from *The Urban Processes* by L. Reissman Copyright (c) by The Free Press of Glencoe, a Division of The Macmillan Company, 1964 and to Routledge and Kegan Paul, Ltd, for permission to adapt two tables from *The Sociology of an English Village: Gosforth* by W.M. Williams (1956).

We also wish to thank the following who have supplied illustrations from which the figures in this book have been prepared:
University of Wales Press for figure 2 taken from an essay by Emrys Jones in *Welsh Rural Communities* edited by E. Davies and A.D. Rees, 1960; Routledge and Kegan Paul Ltd. for figures 7 and 8 taken from *City Region and Regionalism* by R.E. Dickinson, 1947; *Geographical Review* for figure 10 from an article by J.E. Brush and H.E. Bracey in the *Geographical Review* Vol 45, 1955, copyrighted by the American Geographical Society of New York; H.E. Bracey and *Economic Geography* for figure 12 taken from an article in *Economic Geography* 32, 1956; The Controller of Her Majesty's Stationery Office and R.J. Green for figure 17 taken from *Planning Bulletin 8 – Settlement in the Countryside and Country Planning: the future of the rural regions* (1971).

Foreword

Over the past seven years I have been privileged to assist very many mature students in acquiring a greater appreciation of the sociology of rural life. These have been predominantly agricultural advisers and rural development workers from Britain and overseas. One of their prime concerns has been to gain a deeper insight into the processes of change, especially at local levels, so as to be able to act purposefully and efficiently in developmental change and an enhanced wellbeing among the rural people in their areas of work. Although this small book is concerned primarily with Britain, it reflects this bias in my own teaching; I make no apology for it. Most rural sociologists, of whom relatively few exist in the United Kingdom, recognise that the nature of social change among rural and agricultural peoples forms the core of their subject today.

In addition to expressing my thanks in general to all my past students, I am happy to acknowledge the particular assistance of three in constructing Figure 11, namely John Ward, Tony Poole and Michael Kelsey who provided the information on Norfolk, Suffolk and Essex respectively. I am also grateful to Mrs Shirley Green for the extremely efficient and painstaking secretarial work in typing the manuscript. Finally, I am most indebted to Margaret, my wife, for all her encouragment and unflagging forbearance. All inadequacies and errors are, of course, my own responsibility.

GWYN E. JONES

What is 'rural'? 1

It is commonly stated that every Englishman is a countryman at heart. Similar claims are also made for the rurality of the Welsh, the Scots and the Irish—on the whole with a good deal more justification than for the majority of contemporary English people. To dream and sing of a green and pleasant land, to delight in a rural heritage, albeit without giving too much thought to the people who live and work in the countryside, may be a necessary antidote to the urban environment which is home to the majority of the nation's population. The rural myth has been fondly nurtured for many decades, supported by many social and commercial devices, even to the picturesque village churches, thatched cottages and rose gardens portrayed on innumerable calendars and chocolate boxes.

The real situation is rarely this. A few villages win well-deserved 'Best Kept Village' awards from their county rural community council; the bases of such attainments usually rest in the personal and local pride of their inhabitants. Most British villages, however, would hardly attract any attention from artists, tourists, or chocolate box manufacturers. The commoner picture is either one which contains many old cottages and terraced houses in a state of physical decay, or one in which recent estates of suburban-type dwellings have been attached to, and become at least physically a part of existing villages. This ordinariness in the appearance of villages, although no two are identical and all are changing, is usually matched by the normality of the social life within them.

This is not meant in any way to disparage the presentday

inhabitants of British villages, their lives, their ways of living, or their homes. Rather, it is merely to stress that rural or village life is no more or less glamorous than urban life. As in the towns, the wellbeing of individual inhabitants, families and of a community depends on access to employment, to services and amenities, on social organisations and relationships, and on the adaptability of the people as individuals and as groups to changing conditions.

In Britain the 'rural society' has attracted much intellectual interest, especially since the end of the eighteenth century. During the past two centuries or so, as the nation progressively became more urban and industrial, much of the inspiration of poets, dramatists and novelists, as well as of musicians and artists, has been derived from the rural scene. In addition, much study during the period, as well as analysis and writing of a more scientific kind, has focused on rural society. Often these writings clearly reflect the authors' political or ideological points of view, and the result has frequently been the expression of what has been termed 'social nostalgia' for a kind of society which changed, a glorification of an imagined past, an attempt to re-create an idyllic peasantry, or the emergence of a 'rural sentimentality' which bore little resemblance to the true situation. This is true from various eighteenth-century poets (such as Oliver Goldsmith's *The Deserted Village*) to the innumerable tracts concerning the virtues of country life which became increasingly common during this century, especially up to the 1930s, and whose popularity has by no means passed.

Some notable exceptions have existed to the romanticised portrayal of British rural life. At the end of the eighteenth century the recently established Board of Agriculture commissioned a *General View of the Agriculture of* . . . each county. These, together with some later revisions, provide a reasonably accurate account of British farming at the time, although their content is somewhat variable concerning the social and economic aspects of farm life. During the course of the nineteenth century, however, periodic concern over the condition of British agriculture and its workers led to several Royal or Parliamentary Commissions which provide a vivid picture of many aspects of contemporary rural life. In the late nineteenth century, many individuals wrote detailed studies of their native localities, especially in Wales, the North of England and Scotland—many of which are invaluable as source material to the local historian today. One of the more detailed local studies in England was a study by Maude Davies of the parish of Crowsley, in West Wiltshire.[1] This investigator in 1906 attempted to apply scientific methods of analysis, methods which had been evolved especially by Booth and Rowntree in their studies of urban life and poverty in East London and York respectively, with the aim of describing the nature of rural poverty. Another influential antidote to the growing sentimentality surrounding rural life was a perceptive desciption by 'George Bourne', published in 1912, of the nature of recent social change in a Surrey village which at the time was beginning to be affected by London workers seeking rural dwellings.[2] But it is only in more recent years, especially since 1940, that detailed studies have been made by social scientists of life in British 'rural communities'.[3]

X Britain today is predominantly an urban nation. The processes of urbanisation and industrialisation, which have a longer history than in most countries, have also reached a more advanced stage. By whatever definition of 'rural' that may be used, the 'rural population' comprises a minority of the total. It can be fairly deduced from the estimates of the population of England and Wales prepared by Gregory King at the close of the seventeenth century that over 75 per cent of the people lived in what might be regarded as rural areas. This was at a time before many of our present larger towns and cities had developed and before much urban industrialisation had occurred; but these trends were already present. By the middle of the nineteenth century about half the population was rural, and by the beginning of this century the proportion had fallen to around 25 per cent. Today, a realistic estimate suggests that approximately 30 per cent of the population of England and Wales may be regarded as living in rural areas— which include much low density residential areas around larger towns and cities as well as the whole of smaller country towns.

3

Other estimates of the size of the rural population are considerably more conservative. Within this rural sector of the population, the farming population now forms only a minority (Fig. 1).

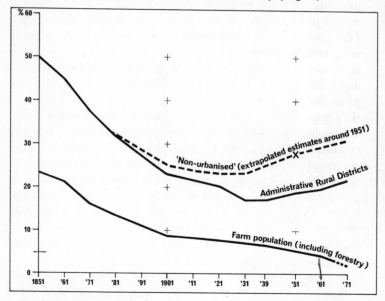

Fig. 1   Proportions of rural population and farm population in England and Wales, 1851–1971

This situation is very different from that in many other countries, particularly the developing countries, and from the situation in the world as a whole. The majority of the world's population today lives in rural areas. Despite a rapid movement of people in many countries from rural areas to the towns and cities, with a declining proportion of the total populations being rural and agricultural, the rate of increase in the total populations is often so rapid that the numbers of rural dwellers continue to increase. Moreover, most of the inhabited surface of the globe is occupied by people living in rural areas; urban population is by definition concentrated and unevenly spread. ✗

Considerable differences in many respects exist between the major continents, and between countries. In North America, well under one-sixth of the population lives in the countryside and settlements of under around 5,000 population; in Africa, four in every five people do so. Even by the end of this century, well over half the populations of Africa and Asia, who will account for about three-quarters of the world's population, is likely to live and work in rural areas. Indeed, a majority of the world's population will probably still be rural. In other words, a rural existence is, and will continue for a long time to be, a major social characteristic of the world's population, specifically in the less developed regions.

Although urbanisation is undoubtedly accelerating in the world as a whole, and forms one of the most important processes carrying along social change, it is also giving rise to immense social, economic and political problems. A significant fact, however, is that very many, often most, of the urban dwellers of the world are first generation residents. Their upbringing, outlook, values and norms, are often rural, and persist as such to a large degree. Often they remain as peasant villagers; 'the villages have been extended into the cities '.[4], [5]

Most of what has been written so far begs the question of what is meant by the term 'rural'. Its use, as that of 'urban', varies widely. Often, the two terms are used (as we have done above) in opposition to each other, suggesting a dichotomy which is essentially fallacious. The core meanings or extreme types implied by each term are generally acceptable—the open remote countryside generally used for agriculture on the one hand, and the large city, cosmopolitan complexes on the other. But when does the rural become the urban? Often, the one merges into the other; they intermix and blend to varying degrees and with differing social results in various countries and cultures.

For some purposes, however, the rural-urban distinction and the ability to separate the one from the other is considered useful. Population censuses usually make the differentiation on the basis of administrative areas which have been delineated as 'rural' or 'urban', or on the basis of the population size of settlements, or

5

according to the population density in small areas. The administrative area distinction has been made in British censuses since the end of the last century, but a special study of the 1951 Population Census data for England and Wales[6] indicated that a division 'in terms of local authorities produces a more "urban" picture than would a more rigorous analysis' (Population Census, 1958). This conclusion was based on a detailed separation of 'rural' from 'urban' areas on the basis of a population density of ten persons per acre (a relatively high *rural* population density).

A more widely used distinction between 'rural' and 'urban' in many countries is according to the lower population limit used to define a 'town'. This varies widely, from a population of 200 in some Scandinavian countries to 10,000 in Greece, with most countries adopting some point between 1,000 and 5,000.[7] But the real nature of an urban, as opposed to a rural environment depends to a large extent on variations in cultural norms. In areas where dispersed settlement was (and to some degree still is) a normal characteristic of the culture, as in Celtic countries, relatively small nucleated settlements have often been considered as towns. On the other hand, where the countryside is densely populated, and where the agricultural population has traditionally lived in nucleated settlements (for example, in much of the Indian sub-continent and parts of the Middle East), villages with populations of many thousands can properly be regarded as 'rural'; in India, a 'town' is officially defined as having a population of at least 5,000, a population density of over 1,000 per square mile, and over 75 per cent of the male adult population being engaged in non-agricultural work.

The United Nations, in attempting a satisfactory international compromise, has accepted Kingsley Davis's view that an indication of the world's urban population can be obtained by considering urban areas as those settlements with 20,000 inhabitants and over. This is widely accepted as erring on the safe side and an over-estimation of the world's rural population; but more detailed studies on a global scale have suggested that a settlement should contain above 10,000 population before it can safely be regarded as 'urban'.

Any distinction between rural and urban should also be viewed in a developmental sense. Social and economic development has invariably, up to the present, involved the growth of towns and cities and an increasing differentiation between the agricultural and non-agricultural sectors of a society. Historically, the trend has been one of a growing difference between the countryside and urban areas in their economic, sociological, demographic and political characteristics. But in industrialised, highly urbanised societies, this trend appears to be becoming reversed—rural–urban differences are becoming less. The meaningful question in such countries, and this is certainly true of Britain, is no longer, is this place or is this community, or are these people rural or urban? but rather, to what extent is this place or people *relatively* rural or urban in character?

To some degree, this removes the need to distinguish between 'rural' and 'urban'. But the conceptual problem of definition remains. Louis Wirth, in a classic paper, has discussed 'urbanism' as a way of life;[8] the same is true of 'ruralism'. Neither is by now merely a matter of place or location. Both are characterised more by ways of thinking and behaviour which are to a greater or less degree different. The two concepts may be viewed as extremities of a series of continua, over which a collection of socio-psychological, sociological, demographic, economic and political traits gradually change.

Any individual, or family, or neighbourhood, or community, may at one and the same time exhibit some characteristics which approach the urban end, while other characteristics are nearer the rural end. The concept of the rural–urban continuum, which is considered in more detail in the next chapter, has enjoyed a considerable if controversial vogue among sociologists; although it has latterly been severely criticised, it can still have considerable value in this multidimensional sense. Moreover, it allows a reconciliation of the rural–urban mixture which is the reality in the countryside's population of a country such as Britain, of the two-way influences between the countryside and the towns and cities, and their interdependence. This can provide a meaningful

7

framework from which to begin a discussion of British rural society. It is not so much which people within our total society are rural that matters, as considering the inhabitants of the countryside and villages (the conventional rural people) in terms of their relative rurality. In Britain today these people and their lives are a blend of numerous rural as well as urban traits.

A conceptual framework

In the systematic study of a society, or any of its sectors, most social scientists would agree that establishing a framework against which the real situation can be viewed is not only helpful but adds meaning to the facts acquired and the understanding achieved. Some may dignify this approach with the claim that it forms their 'theoretical' basis, even if they are not attempting, or have no means to support the validity or otherwise of their theory. It is often more appropriate to regard any framework as a 'model' which, having been constructed on the basis of defined concepts, elements and their relationships, can be tested against the reality, thereby aiming to refine and improve the model.

One noteworthy model, which has been considered significant among rural sociologists, is the 'rural–urban continuum'. Sociologists and anthropologists in their investigations and interpretations of the nature of society, particularly of rural society, have used this model in one or other of its various forms for over a century. Essentially, it is a comparative model which, in the ways it has been used, has aimed to embrace the characteristics which typify and distinguish a 'rural' culture or society from an 'urban'. In some, especially its older forms and their use, the model merely specifies a dichotomy of society into either of the two types, thus stressing the differences and discontinuities between the 'rural' and the 'urban'. Current uses more commonly emphasise the continuum, drawing attention to the gradual changes and transformations which occur from one polar extreme to the other, having in each case outlined the (theoretical) profile of characteristics which typify the extremities. Different terms have been used to indicate the two poles, varying according to the particular sets of concepts, frames of reference and the ranges of attributes with which their various authors have been concerned. Table 1 lists some of the main formulations of a dichotomy or continuum which have been suggested in this context.

TABLE 1

Typologies and continua analogous to the rural–urban continuum.

Author	'Rural' or 'non-urban' terminology	'Urban' terminology
Sir Henry Maine (1861)	Status	Contract
Herbert Spencer (1862)	Military	Industrial
Ferdinand Tönnies (1887)	*Gemeinschaft*	*Gesellschaft*
Emile Durkheim (1893)	Mechanical solidarity	Organic solidarity
Max Weber (1922)*	Traditional	Rational
Robert Redfield (1947)	Folk	Urban
Howard Becker (1950)	Sacred	Secular

*posthumous publication of main works.
Based on a table in Reissman (1964),[1] p. 123.

None of these formulations is specific to any particular cultural situation, nor, except by implication, do any provide an adequate description of the rural or urban sectors of any society. The essence of all, however, either as a dichotomy or as a continuum between 'rural' and 'urban', is to typify the 'rural' pole as an idealised, unchanging peasant society, organised in small, inward-looking, idyllic communities based on kinship and supported by subsistence agriculture. The 'urban' end is the ever-changing life of the large, cosmopolitan, commercial cities.

In recent years, this concept of a rural–urban continuum has been severely criticised (see, for example, references 2, 3, 4). Its critics have shown that the interpretations and uses to which it has been put have often been simplistic. As a result, and some have suggested that this is inherent in the concept of a continuum, it has not been regarded as very meaningful either as a basis for classification or as a research tool; it has led to generalisations which are not only too broad but which are inaccurate, so that in all it is unimportant. Further, particularly when the continuum has been applied to observations or data of an international or cross-cultural kind, it has been criticised as reflecting a degree of Western ethnocentricism and a particular ideological position on the part of some sociologists who have used it. Such an ideological attachment has been clear in the writings of many who have been concerned with rural society; the generalised view of a 'rural' polar type has been equated with a normative type of rural life—the 'ideal-type' has been idealised into what ought to be.

Many of these criticisms are based on assumptions which are not inherent to the concept of a continuum. In particular, users of a continuum have assumed that the descriptions of the polar extremes are universally valid and more or less constant (the latter being assumed especially for the 'rural' end), and that the transformation occurring along the continuum is necessarily continuous and 'linear'. Many interpreters and users of the continuum have unquestioningly accepted these assumptions, and have consequently proceeded to ignore a great deal of the variety which exists not only between societies but also within a society among social groups who appear to be, in crude terms, at more or less similar points along the continuum. Many critics, however, have been aware that it is the use of the continuum in this way which is invalid, rather than the ideas of the original formulators of the various forms of continuum. As Hauser states: 'most of the scholars who contributed to the emergence of these concepts regarded them not as generalisations based on research, but, rather, as "ideal-type constructs" ', but 'the widespread acceptance of these ideal-type constructs as generalisations, without the benefit of adequate research, well illustrates the dangers of catchy neologisms which often get confused with knowledge'.[5] Loomis,[6] referring specifically to Tönnies's treatise,[7] states: 'No social system could persist if relations were either completely *Gemeinschaft*-like or completely *Gesellschaft*-like. This fact does not prevent the human mind from conceiving of such "ideal types" and using them for comparative and ordering purposes. In fact this is their chief value.'

Despite the fact that the rural–urban continuum remains an object of controversy among social scientists (see, for example, references 4, 8, 9 and 10), it retains a value as a framework within which to explore and interpret the nature and variations of a defined social system. It was implicit in much of the writings of the originators of the various forms of the continuum that the descriptions they gave of the polar positions were intended to be of hypothetical and ideal types. Against these, real social situations could be assessed according to the extent or relative degree to which they resembled either pole. The continuum can therefore act either as a basis for classifying, or as a framework for discussing, recent trends and an indicator of future social change (the continuum representing a process), or for both purposes.

Moreover, for all the original authors, the ideal type at each pole contained a collection of characteristics. There is, indeed, much in common between the various characteristics included in the different formulations. In a very real sense, therefore, the rural–urban continuum may be considered as composed of a cluster of continua, each representing one of a variety of characteristics. The relevance and relative dominance of the characteristics included vary in different cultural situations; all need not be present in every circumstance. In addition, the meaning of a particular characteristic, present in a certain quantity, quality or form, differs in dissimilar settings according to the varied nature of the other social characteristics present, while the transformation of each characteristic along its continuum is unlikely to occur in an identical way to the change in any other characteristic (i.e. the continua may neither be parallel to each other nor necessarily 'linear'). Above all, however, the concept of the continuum allows one to embrace the idea that any social system can be classified in relation to others, and that its changing nature, as a result of alterations in its characteristics, is not only complex but can also be comprehended in relation to changes in other systems and the relative changes occurring in its own various characteristics.

Of the several classic formulations of a continuum which are analogous to the rural–urban continuum, the one which has had most influence on the thinking of rural sociologists has been that of Tönnies. In developing the contrast between a *Gemeinschaft* and a *Gesellschaft*, Tönnies drew his examples and applied his concepts in the context of sub-units within a society—social groups and relationships. The main feature of the two types are outlined in Table 2.

TABLE 2
Major characteristics of Gemeinschaft *and* Gesellschaft.

Social characteristics	Gemeinschaft	Gesellschaft
Dominant social relationships based on:	kinship, locality and neighbourliness, fellowship, – a sharing of responsibilities and fates, and a furtherance of mutual good through familiarity and under-standing, and the exercise and consensus of 'natural' wills or sentiment in evaluations, assessments and decisions. 'Common goods – common evils; common friends – common enemies' (p. 50)*.	exchange, rational calculation, specific function, – formal and limited responsibilities, and a furtherance of personal good through the exercise of rational wills and validated knowledge. ' . . . everybody is by himself and isolated, and there exists a condition of tension against all others' (p. 65)*.
Ordering of social institutions:	family life, rural village life, town life	city life, national life, cosmopolitan life
Characteristic form of wealth:	land	money
Central institutions and forms of social control:	family law, extended kinship group, concord, customs and mores, religion	the state, convention, contracts, political legislation, public opinion
Status-role:	everyone's role fully integrated in the system, the status of each being ascribed	role based on each specific relationship, the status in each being based on personal achievement

*quotations from Loomis's translation.

It is the emphasis on social relationships, and the associated institutions and personal roles at the level of meaningful social groups, such as the family and the village, which have made it an attractive base for rural sociological work. The *Gemeinschaft* has been regarded as the extreme 'rural community,—remembering that in Tönnies's formulation it is an ideal-type. It also allows somewhat easier connections than several other continuum formulations with recent theories of social action and social change at a local level, which arise largely from individual status and role within the context of meaningful social groups.

SOCIAL ELEMENTS AND PROCESSES

A person's 'status' and 'role' within his social system may be taken as a starting point for a brief discussion of the elements and processes of a relevant social system (such as a village, a rural community, or any permanent social group). Status implies a position within a system which affects and is affected by an individual's prestige (gained from the position he occupies) and his esteem (enjoyed by virtue of his performance in one or more roles).[11] Role implies a process, the behaviours to be expected from an individual in a particular relationship. Due to the obviously close connections between the two concepts, there is much to commend their combination into one element, 'status-role'.[12] This draws attention away from the psychological aspects of an individual's role, while it focuses on reciprocal expectancies in the context of meaningful social relationships. Status-role is thus the pattern of actions (and reactions) expected of an individual who occupies a given position, which attracts rewards or punishments from others in such a way that the individual's status position is reinforced or enhanced, or is weakened or reduced, according to how well he lives up to the expectations of others. For example, a 'good farmer' in a particular locality may be expected by his friends and neighbours (those who give him this status position) to react to technical innovations and their advocates in a particular way, possibly with cautious scepticism;

any different behaviour on his part would be to risk a loss of status.

In an extreme, ideal-type, rural situation, it has been suggested[13] that a low density of role texture exists, that is, an individual's roles are broadly defined, undifferentiated and diffuse, involving functions which at one and the same time may have kinship, economic, political, religious and ritual, and recreational connotations. By contrast, in the urban ideal-type, roles are highly specific and specialised, producing a high density of role texture. In the former, role relationships are likely to be longstanding, and therefore affective, with considerable overlapping between an individual's various roles; in the latter, relationships are ephemeral based on discrete roles. This is in keeping with the *Gemeinschaft—Gesellschaft* typology. It also bears a close resemblance to aspects of the continua involved in Parson's pattern variables of action orientation.[14]

Given that a rural ideal-type is also conceived as consisting of permanent small groups, of close-knit, stable populations which lack both geographical and social mobility, an individual's status is total. This arises from his position being ascribed and from the summation of his roles (and his performance of them). A complete way of life is embraced, which is common to the group, with the individual's actions being orientated inevitably towards the group and its continuity. The beliefs and values, as well as the norms of social behaviour and activities within the group, are thus not only maintained, but also controlled and continuously reinforced, which in turn confirms the existing structure. It is not what one does which is important, as much as *how* one does something because one is who one is; and 'who one is' is a matter of an internal assessment of status, rather than of rank or one's position in a stratification based on achievements and standards evaluated externally to the group. This conception of the ideal-type rural community thus implies a closed, integrated, complex group, isolated socially from (or at least oblivious of) the larger society; communication with the outside world, or linkages with other social systems, are at best very limited. (For a further discussion and very clear analysis of 'rural' and 'less rural' social systems, see references 15, part 2; 16; and 17, chs. 2 and 7.)

It would be foolish to expect that any British rural community or village is identical to this ideal-type. Indeed, as the critics of the rural-urban continuum have rightly stressed, nowhere is like this. But, the ideal-type forms a base against which the actual can be compared. Within the rural areas of Britain today, considerable differences occur. Compared to the past, even to the early part of this century, considerable change has occurred. Rural communities generally were much more *Gemeinschaft*-like seventy years ago. Compared with the present, they were considerably more isolated socially and self-contained economically, although considerable variation existed between villages and rural areas.

Recent surveys and other data have indicated that in several respects rural dwellers today are little different from their urban counterparts. Birth and death rates are very similar in rural and urban areas (in terms of administrative areas). Certain causes of death and the incidence of infectious diseases are lower in the countryside, but differences between certain areas in Britain are generally of more importance (ref. 17, ch. 3). Although agriculture by now provides a livelihood for a very low proportion of the population, it is clearly of more importance in the occupational structure of rural areas.

The attachment of people to 'a place' as their home is of considerable sociological significance. In general, the ability of people to conceive of a particular area as their 'home area', although it increases (as might be anticipated) with length of residence, is similar in general between cities, towns and rural areas. Moreover, the varying lengths of residence by people in their area, which reflects the pattern of geographical mobility and the feeling of 'belonging' to the area, in the sense that all or most relatives and friends also live in the locality, are similar in town and country (Table 3). These findings, and those in the following two paragraphs, are based on a random national survey of 'community attitudes' in England, conducted in 1967[18]; they are on the whole borne out by several more local surveys.

TABLE 3
Similarities between rural and urban inhabitants in their conceptions of a 'home' locality

	Rural districts	Municipal boroughs and urban districts	County boroughs
Numbers of respondents in sample	358	190	751
	percentages		
Ability to conceptualise a 'home' area	76	80	76
Length of residence in 'home' area:			
up to 3 years	16	16	14
over 3, up to 10 years	23	23	21
over 10, up to 20 years	18	19	21
over 20 years	28	24	28
born here and continuous residence	15	18	16
All or most relatives/friends living in 'home' area:			
relatives	14	20	14
friends	39	41	36

Source: Royal Commission on Local Government in England (1969)[18], Tables 1, 26 and 44.

However, the extent of the area which is regarded as 'home' tends to be larger in rural areas, while the inhabitants more frequently claim to know 'many' more other people in this area than do city dwellers. In addition, in a day to day sense, rural people (especially young adults) are more mobile than their urban counterparts: they travel more often outside their home area to work, for shopping, for recreation and entertainment, and, in the case of children, to school. This reflects both the relative lack of opportunities and facilities in the villages (which have often deteriorated significantly in recent years) and the ability of country dwellers to travel. Ownership or access to a motor vehicle is generally higher in rural areas, although a substantial proportion of residents still rely on public transport. This has progressively worsened in most rural areas, especially those remote from larger towns and cities in the post-war period, and the elderly and lower income households in rural communities are thus often at a considerable disadvantage; this is a problem which has received considerable attention in recent years leading to changes and relaxations in official regulations concerning passenger-carrying vehicles.

The research report on which much of this is based states that 'a very slight tendency is visible for greater interest in the area to be shown as one moves along the CB—MB/UD—RD continuum' (p. 28). This is not only based on statements by individuals concerning their personal interest in local activities, but is also reflected in their participation in organisations in their home area and their composite involvement in local affairs (Table 4). A

TABLE 4

Differences in interest in the 'home' locality and its affairs between rural and urban inhabitants

	Rural districts	Municipal boroughs and urban districts	County boroughs
	percentages		
Degree of interest in what goes on in 'home' area:			
very interested and quite interested	62	57	49
only a little interested	26	27	29
not at all interested	11	16	21
don't know	1	–	1
Belonging to one or more organisations in 'home' area	43	41	32
Overall interest and involvement in local affairs:			
high	23	16	13
medium	45	45	46
low	32	39	41

Source: Royal Commission on Local Government in England (1969)[18], Tables 22, 55 and 174.

picture thus emerges of the inhabitants of rural localities as being on the whole more socially active than their urban counterparts, and that over a larger geographical space; they are not generally isolated, or inward-looking. Despite being increasingly more in contact with, and open to the influences of, urban ways of life, in which the mass media play a crucial part, and less attached to norms associated with the traditional village community, the inhabitants of rural Britain are thus still different from the urban dwellers.

But at any one time, an immense diversity exists among our rural communities, as much if not more than in many other countries. The primary interes in this book is with the social diversity which exists within the rural sector. A simple dichotomy between 'rural' and 'urban' is too crude a model to comprehend this. Rather, it is legitimate to seek understanding from a relevant part of a rural–urban continuum.

A SOCIAL TYPOLOGY OF VILLAGES

Twenty years ago, on the basis of detailed studies of a selection of Devon villages, Mitchell proposed a useful typology of village communities.[19], [20] This is compatible with the concept of a continuum as discussed earlier. It is based on two broad sets of factors which do not necessarily vary directly with each other: (a) an open—closed community, and (b) an integrated—lack of integration or disintegrating community. Both suggest the processes involved. By 'open' is meant that the community is receptive to change arising from influences originating outside the local social system which affect it, i.e., systemic linkage is dominant as opposed to boundary maintenance. 'Integrated' implies a relatively high degree of internal harmony, as opposed to conflict, overt deviancy from norms and lack of consistency in the allocation of roles.

A combination of these two sets of criteria produces four general types, viz: 1. open, integrated; 2. closed, integrated; 3. open, lacking integration; 4. closed, disintegrating. Mitchell was able to distinguish villages of each of these types within a relatively small area, and the typology is certainly still valid and applicable in considering rural communities in Britain as a whole. Inevitably, the boundaries between the types are somewhat indeterminate, as the one merges into another, while over time, a community may change its character (as a result of internal social change, or of external forces acting upon it, especially planning decisions) and consequently its type.

The *open, integrated* rural community is usually relatively large, with a diversity of occupations and displaying in its institutional and organisational framework an adaptability towards changing conditions. It is often the social and economic centre for several surrounding villages. Within it, a relatively large proportion of inhabitants are involved in local affairs, initiative being shown in various ways. People are generally ready to accept duties and responsibilities. The community is thus relatively self-sufficient socially, and a general feeling exists that it is an active, proud community. Various links are maintained with the larger society without leading to a feeling that this could in any way be a hazard to the community's continuance. Although Mitchell sees this type as resembling a suburban society, a large number of villages in areas very distant from the larger towns and cities exhibit these characteristics to a high degree.

The *closed, integrated* community is one which is able to remain more or less isolated, with a relatively stable population. Although it may be variable in size, it is broadly inward-looking, self-contained and traditional (in the attitudes of its inhabitants, its mode of life and leadership), maintaining firm boundaries against outside influences. Roles are well-defined and the range of norms of social behaviour is relatively narrow. This is reflected in attitudes, for example, towards any newcomers or to external institutions (such as politics or national sport), which are often reinforced by its religious organisation. Despite the inevitable penetration of numerous urban influences via the mass media, this type of community still exists, and it is by no means confined, as might be imagined, to the remoter areas of the country.

A community which is *open but lacking in integration* is invariably affected by changes at a rate which it cannot assimilate. In many instances, this arises from a rapidly growing population. The commuter or dormitory villages, as well as many new industrial villages where this is occurring are in most cases the result of accretions on to existing villages. To this extent, the type of the village has changed. Due to their growth as a result of the inflow of population as well as, often, a high rate of population turnover, their common characteristics are an instability in any organisations, and a lack of civic responsibility and leadership. The external linkages are invariably greater than the internal bonds; internally, tensions and conflicts are common. It is almost, but not quite completely, an outward-looking community. New social ideas may be enthusiastically received, but dissensions among the new-comers, or between the newcomers and the original inhabitants, commonly lead to their discontinuance. In a very real sense, they appear as a kind of suburbia transferred to a rural setting.

The *closed, disintegrating* rural community is generally small and decreasing in size. It has been unable to adapt to change, or has resisted it. Often, the decreased labour requirements in agriculture, or the closure of a local source of employment, may have initiated the process. But the resulting loss of population has led to a remaining number which is too small to maintain a viable village economy. The result is likely to be a progressive worsening in services, facilities and amenities, often hastened by planning decisions, with a feeling of helplessness among the remaining inhabitants. This type of decaying village community is common in the older industrial areas in many parts of the country.

Rural ways of life in Britain

Rural life in Britain exhibits tremendous variety, as already indicated. No two villages, rural communities or localities are identical. Yet it is one aim of a social scientist to attempt meaningful generalisations, not at an absurd level of suggesting a sameness and a homogeneity in rural life which would be palpably false, but in terms that may clarify certain patterns and processes.

It might appear that the urban influences on the rural environment are invariably disruptive and create disorganisation. Mitchell's closed yet disintegrating type of community, which is unable to develop and adapt to modern economic, political and technological forces, as much as the open community which lacks integration due to the rate of change being too rapid for its assimilation, both imply this. But rural communities which are on the whole integrated are also common. This is in no sense a result of possessing an immunity to the total society and its predominantly urban values. In all cases, an interaction occurs to varying degrees; a great deal of the change taking place in such rural communities arises from it. A complex process of interaction appears to be common universally in rural areas, even to the extent that it can be convincingly argued as the basis of a contemporary 'rural revolution' all over the world.[1]

The result by today in developed countries such as Britain is that many of the traditional features which distinguished rural from urban life are disappearing. 'In the most advanced societies the differences between urban and rural, excepting the physical milieu of each, are rapidly disappearing; the exception is being steadily narrowed, in the densely populated countries, by the increasing invasion of the countryside by bricks and mortar'.[2] 'There are good reasons to believe that the climax of this differentiation process between city and country has already been passed in the industrial societies, and the trend is toward a comprehensive urbanisation of non-urban areas. ... Urbanism is no longer a matter of geographical location, something confined to urban places. It is characterised by a certain mentality and way of behaving.'[3] The urban influences on the countryside are comprehensive, from the physical to the psychological. But the linkages are not created or maintained purely by an urban initiative. Rural dwellers often seek the connections, in terms of their work, services and recreation. To a degree, the interactions are mutually reinforcing, as we shall discuss later.

The linkages between rural communities and the larger society affect their internal character in numerous ways. But their present condition, and any changes occurring within them, are also a result of their internal characteristics. Sociological distinctions always exist *within* rural communities; a complete social homogeneity is inconceivable, except as a characteristic of an ideal type. Any internal distinctions may merge gradually into each other, although marked discontinuities may also exist. It is not only the nature of internal distinctions which is important, however, but also the evaluative criteria which are used by the community's inhabitants for defining the differences. These criteria change as a community's characteristics alter, while the differences and the bases perceived for them imply degrees of internal tension, discernible in varying behaviour patterns, social norms and values among the inhabitants, and these, in turn, affect further change.

LOCAL 'COMMUNITY' STUDIES IN RURAL BRITAIN

A long tradition has existed in Britain whereby local inhabitants (usually) have published historical accounts and descriptions of life in their localities at the time of writing. This tradition still continues, and in recent years some organisations, notably the Women's Institute movement, have stimulated such endeavours.

23

The majority of such writings have been concerned with rural areas and, used with discretion, they provide much useful historical information, although their thoroughness and accuracy varies. During the past thirty years, however, a much clearer understanding of several rural localities has emerged from more detailed, scientific studies.

Some of these have been of a socio-economic kind, generally emphasising certain overt structures, such as the occupations, economy, services, organisations and population movements of an area, and its problems (see, for example, references 4, 5, 6, 7). Others, undertaken usually by social anthropologists or sociologists, have been concerned to analyse the sociological characteristics and variations within rural communities. For the main published ones see references 8–18.

It is not practical to summarise these 'community studies' in one chapter; for short summaries of 8, 10, and 11 see Frankenberg (Ch. 2, ref. 15). Students should strive to read several—they are interesting reading—so as to be able to place against them their own knowledge or observations of rural localities and their inhabitants, and as examples of the methods which can be employed to study small communities. They also indicate the kind of understanding which investigators, each with their own predispositions concerning what features are of interest to them, can achieve by detailed local studies. That the facts they contain are progressively becoming more out-of-date is much less important than the ways in which various concepts have been used in order to interpret the life of the communities concerned.

Each author has been interested in a specific village, locality or area, largely as an entity in itself. These have been chosen not so much in order to test general hypotheses (such as recent change as an indicator of urbanisation in rural areas) as to describe and analyse salient characteristics of the social structure at the time of the study, usually with reference to the longer-term changes which have occurred in the area. The greater number of these studies have been in remoter areas of the country. Their number and geographical distribution is certainly inadequate to generalise on regional differences in rural life, but they do form an invaluable basis from which (however inadequately) to consider certain sociological features of rural communities.

Various methods have been used to interpret the way of life in a rural community. For example, the emphasis may be placed on a dominant institution (such as kinship, religion or recreation) which displays a community's structure in a concentrated form by amplifying the internal differences; or on people's behaviour and actions (as reflected in their cooperation with each other, or their participation in social activities, or other facets of their ways of living); or on inhabitants' backgrounds and social origins, and their effects on their associations with other people. Each approach has a relevance which may be more or less significant in different circumstances—the diagnosis of which aspects are most crucial implies an art, as well as a science, which a successful investigator of a community exhibits to a high degree. But, in all cases, it is a matter of emphasis since the various facets of a community's social structure intertwine in numerous ways.

Kinship connections, and the family to which one belongs, are invariably of significance in a rural community; this has been emphasised in most of the community studies to which reference has been made. In particular, in agriculture the family is not only the unit living on the farm, but it commonly provides most of the labour required. It is thus the dominant production unit, and is the basis for all considerations regarding the property and its inheritance (see Williams[14] for an example of the ramifications of this in detail). Among the non-farming population, one's family can also be crucial in the social assessment of an individual's position, or his right to occupy a certain position, in the community.

In stable communities, especially if they are relatively closed and integrated, kinship connections can form a dense network which links a large proportion of the inhabitants. This was shown to a marked degree by Rees[8] (ch. 6) in his study of Llanfihangel yng Ngwynfa in the 1940s. To a greater or less degree this is true in most rural localities (see, for example, Williams,[10] ch. 3), and even where kinship may not be a dominant feature, it is

25

commonly of considerable significance among those who form the stable element of the population and have lived there a long time; a good example of this situation is in Eskdalemuir, as shown in Littlejohn's study (Littlejohn[13], pp. 6–10). It is undoubtedly true that the institution of kinship is less dominant today than in the past, if only as a result of the greater geographical mobility of rural people, but family connections still matter in rural communities. Particularly in those areas outside the immediate impact of the larger towns and cities (where new residents of urban origin have become very numerous, and possibly a majority in the population), kinship can frequently emerge as a dominating force. Cooperation (or the lack of it) among particular families, allegiances to local social organisations, and informal communication within a community (the gossip networks, including their existence at all) often depend on kinship connections. These connections become obvious at major occurrences in the life of a family (such as weddings, funerals, or serious illness). Loudon[19] has shown the significance which the extended family still has in the Vale of Glamorgan, and the relationship of kinship to the gossip networks and to friendship and neighbourhood groups. One of the major problems invariably facing newcomers and their integration into a rural locality is their lack of knowledge of the kinship links among the long established residents.

Even in a large urbanised village such as Wigston Magna (Elias and Scotson[18]), one's family and the network of relationships and other connections among the old-established families can be important in determining the character of the community, the extent of cohesion within it, and who gains political positions. This may even be more obvious in such circumstances than in smaller, more rural villages. The social reaction to the needs of a village to make its voice heard in local government councils or to decide on a course of action may be reflected in the concerted effect of some section of the population to elect one of themselves. This can arise especially from a consensus among the old-established members of the community if they feel that what to them appear to be large numbers of newcomers are a threat to their own positions. However, where the internal established order is felt to be secure, where outsiders, strangers or newcomers are at best a small minority, it is these who may be placed into formal positions—if things go well, they will have done no harm; otherwise they can be blamed without adversely affecting the cohesion in the community structure (see Frankenberg[11]). In Gosforth, for example, a strong concentration of the titular positions in village organisations occurs in what Williams[10] terms the 'upper-upper class', most of whom are outsiders to the village (Table 5). Even

TABLE 5
Proportions of positions in Gosforth organisations, and of the total population, according to social class

Social class	President, vice-president, chairman, vice-chairman	Secretary, treasurer	Committee member	Total population
	percentages			
Upper-upper	54	2	5	3
Lower-upper	8	–	4	3
Intermediate	10	10	4	1
Total upper class	72	12	13	7
Upper-medial	6	24	13	4
Medial	12	45	38	31
Lower-medial	10	19	35	53
Lower	–	–	1	5
Total lower class	28	88	87	93
Total	100	100	100	100*
Total number of positions	51	42	164	Total Population = 723

*based on 694 of the population for whom class position was determined. Derived from Williams (1956)[10] Fig. 7, p. 125 and Appendix V, Table 5, p. 217.

so, it is significant that the key positions of secretary and treasurer in the organisations are held by individuals who are much more

27

representative of the population as a whole; this is a phenomenon which appears to be usual in rural communities.

The structure of local formal organisations as a whole thus reflects, to a large degree, the structure of the community. The same is true in more informal aspects of life, whether or not attached to a formal organisation, such as who sits next to whom in a village committee, or in church or chapel, who associates with whom at a village activity such as a dance or fete, or who regard each other as friends. But to stress 'class' distinctions in village communities is to emphasise social and interpersonal evaluations based on socioeconomic criteria (basically occupation, income and educational background). These criteria are important, probably increasingly so, and are certainly dominant in larger, more urbanised villages. They should not be allowed to conceal, however, more subtle criteria which operate within smaller communities based on role and normative behaviour.

All the community studies indicate that a 'class' position held by an individual or a family is more than merely a matter of overt characteristics. People also see each other as 'affected', 'snobbish', 'putting on airs', or 'kind and friendly', 'natural', 'decent', or 'selfish', 'dirty', 'ne'er do well', 'no self respect', etc. To know one's neighbours in these ways is to judge them in terms suggesting superiority, or equality, or inferiority, which are based on far more than a superficial knowledge and acquaintance, and which are not necessarily connected with their economic position. Thus it is the social structural element of status-role which can be regarded as dominant in determining distinctions which inhabitants in a rural community perceive among themselves. Even when marked class differences (in an economic sense) exist, interactions among people can override them. For example, a position in the community may attract a high prestige yet be occupied by a person who would be low in any scale of class rankings as a result of being accorded high respect and esteem by others in the community. It is not uncommon for a farm worker to be a chapel deacon in a Welsh locality, or the leading player in an English village cricket team, and the more *Gemeinschaft*-like the community the more likely is the high esteem enjoyed in one sphere of activity to carry over to others. Moreover, individuals or families can gain or lose 'credit', and thus acquire higher or lower status in the total regard with which they are held in a community, on the basis of the relationship between their actual and their expected behaviour in particular activities. Such status can be maintained or acquired both by virtue of activities which are completely internal to the community and as a result of an ability to obtain a certain standing for the community as a whole (or a group within it) vis-à-vis other communities or groups. Invariably it is attached to activities associated with institutions or organisations which are valued by the community, status-role thus being one prime indicator of the inhabitants' values system.

Among farmers in a locality, who are frequently relatively distinct from neighbouring non-farming families (even when their farmsteads are situated within a village), reputation is similarly based on more than family background, farm size and income. Generally of more importance is their way of life, their treatment of their workers (including family members), their relative skill and ability in farming, and whether they can be regarded as 'good' farmers—however that may be assessed locally. For all inhabitants, the ways in which they behave and act as individuals toward each other, whatever their age or sex, will determine the respect both they, and usually their families, are accorded. Within a community there is invariably a configuration of behaviour to which an individual is expected, more or less, to conform, arising from his known background and upbringing, which is reinforced every time he acts as expected; any marked deviation will either injure or, more rarely, improve his repute, and through him that of his family.

This is illustrated most clearly in two of the Welsh community studies, although it is also apparent in the most urbanised village communities. In Wigston Magna (Elias and Scotson[18]) and in the commuter villages in Hertfordshire studied by Pahl[16] the native residents expected the newcomers to behave in certain ways, so that in the view of the former the status of any further outsiders is also, to a large degree, thus predetermined. Conversely, the newcomers have come to expect certain kinds of relationships and reactions from the native villagers. In Aberporth, Jenkins[12] has indicated the existence of two groups within the local community, two distinct ways of living (for which he uses the old Welsh concept *buchedd*). One group's values were based on religion, being teetotal, thrifty, and with a high regard for educating their children as a means of 'getting on in the world'; the other group were pubgoers, considered Sunday as a time for secular recreation, were spendthrift and tended to ridicule education. Although these two *buchedd* groups were associated with some differences in socioeconomic characteristics, the crucial distinction was based on the behaviour patterns of individuals and families. Newcomers to the village were also, on the whole, absorbed into one or other group according to their activities and behaviours.

In Tregaron, a large Welsh village, regarded locally as a town, again a community in which religious behaviour is of paramount importance, Jones[12] has shown how this largely determines status positions. Figure 2 (derived from this study) summarises the situation in a simple manner where a non-religious person, however high his class position in terms of occupation, cannot achieve the highest status in the community. Comparable structural situations exist within most British rural communities, although the number of behavioural configurations which exist in a locality, their components, and the dominant institution may differ. They form the basis on which people are able to assess each other, and do. A cohesiveness in the community, which is apparent when viewed from the outside, and which though real is by no means absolute, is paradoxically maintained internally to a large extent by the distinctions and the degrees of stress and tension which exist between various status groupings. The social structure, as well as change within a rural community, only becomes fully comprehensible in these terms.

The reality of a rural community is also a reflection of the similarities and differences which its inhabitants feel exist between themselves and a wider social environment, which includes other

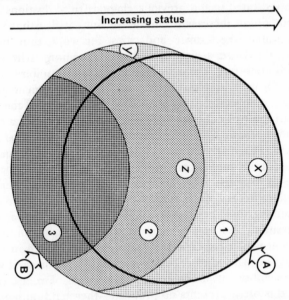

Increasing status

Fig. 2   A diagrammatic representation of status within a community.
Key.   A religious adherents
       B non-religious element
       1 administrative, professional, managerial and proprietor
         category
       2 craftsmen and specialised worker category
       3 unskilled workers and labourers category
Individual x is of higher status than y, although both are in category
1, because x is in A and y in B. Individual z is of higher status than y
although z is in category 2, because z is in A and y in B

rural areas as well as less rural localities and urban centres. This implies both an absorption of a village community into the larger society as well as various tensions which exist between them. However 'closed' a rural community may appear, however firmly it attempts to maintain social boundaries between itself and an outside world, the contemporary nature of a society such as Britain's involves more and more social linkages. In an everyday sense as indicated in the previous chapter, rural dwellers initiate and maintain an increasing number of links with country towns and accessible larger towns and cities, for work, education and pleasure. The larger society as a whole also requires such connections and thus forges and maintains growing numbers of them through the activities of central and local government agencies and their employees, the trading methods of commercial companies, and the impact of national, regional, or county organisations and institutions, among which the Press, radio and television are major influences. To a marked degree, rural and urban people can choose to participate in similar activities and ways of living.

Some rural individuals, families and groups maintain a much greater 'localiteness' or 'parochial-mindedness' in their lives than others among their neighbours. This is another basis of internal differentiation. But among many rural dwellers, an ambivalence is apparent which indicates their uncertainty as much in relaxing their hold on what they regard as normal village or rural ways of life as in embracing urban behaviour patterns. For the younger people, this often presents no problem—they tend (although this is by no means uniformly strong among them) to seek urban ways. For many of the elderly, the changing nature of society, as it is reflected in their rural area, is often incomprehensible, and they firmly align themselves with known, well-established village ways. It is among the manual workers and smaller businessmen (whether farmers, craftsmen or retailers) that the problem is often felt most intensely. Some live in almost two worlds, an urban style and maybe location of work, but a village and rural behaviour in all other respects. For some the problem is resolved by moving to live in a town; much of the permanent physical mobility from rural to urban areas occurs among employed manual workers.

Feelings of distinctions, however, persist between countryfolk and town dwellers. It may be expressed in the disparaging views and opinions which townspeople might express regarding villagers, of which the villager is invariably aware, although such opinions and their underlying attitudes are increasingly less pronounced among those urban dwellers who decide to live in or to regularly visit rural areas. In addition, country people, in various ways, are often made aware of being relatively deprived in comparison to townsfolk, not only in terms of the services and activities in their village, but also in various sociopsychological ways which reflect a variety of factors from physical isolation to income levels and cost of living. The rural dweller at least feels and believes, and to that extent 'knows', that he and his family are often worse off than his urban counterpart in innumerable social as well as economic ways.

One reaction is to reinforce their own identity. Several of the rural community studies indicate that the people express a solidarity vis-à-vis other local communities, which often include local towns (Williams[10]; Frankenberg[11]; Jenkins[12]). But, increasingly, rural communities also exhibit various signs of becoming more diverse and outward-looking, more integrated into larger social areas. An intense internal cohesiveness has generally been eroded; extreme degrees of internal integration are becoming less common. In concluding his study of Eskdalemuir, Littlejohn[13] (p. 155) typifies the locality as

> less 'an area of common life', than an area within which the individual chooses his associations subject to such barriers as are imposed by social class or physical distance. The people round him are no longer all actual neighbours but only possible neighbours. The locale itself ceases to be the actual place where he lives and has his being and becomes one possible place amongst others, to be compared and evaluated with others.

This is a kind of situation which is undoubtedly true, and increasingly so, of very many British rural communities.

Yet such localities, whether they be villages under intense urban pressures near large cities with increasing numbers of commuters as residents, or more remote and still basically agricultural communities, retain a distinctiveness. In part, the small size of the population in a rural locality imposes patterns of

33

interpersonal relationships which affect the status, the prestige, esteem and respect, enjoyed by an individual (and thereby, usually, his family). In part, it is due to the agricultural basis of a great deal of the economic, social and political life of most rural communities. In part, and to an increasing extent, it is also due to the wish of inhabitants, often newcomers as much as old-established residents, to retain or to evolve alternative styles of life to those which they believe exist in urban areas.

Rural social structure and organisation
I. Family and neighbourhood

The variety which persists in British rural society implies that a simple dichotomy between rural and urban cannot be supported. By the second half of the twentieth century there is much overlapping and coalescence between rural and urban life, based on numerous linkages or connections between the countryside and the towns, although various separations also persist. The situation is rarely one of complete dependence by a rural area on an urban; rather, as in the past, there prevails and will continue to exist an interdependence, its character changing continuously in response to social, economic, political and technological changes at all levels, from the national to the local.

One of the most pronounced social features of all rural areas is their relatively low population density. Within Britain this is higher than in many countries, but a considerable variation occurs, from areas in the highlands and uplands which are virtually uninhabited to lowland areas with a dense distribution of villages and hamlets, each in view of one or more others, where the population in an area of ten square miles or so might be well in excess of 2,000. Throughout this range, the landscape would be immediately recognisable as 'rural'. Even the inclusion of a small market town with a population of under 10,000 is unlikely to destroy an area's essential rurality.

The rural landscape of Britain is above all a human habitat. Apart from the settlements, the land is used more or less intensively, largely for agriculture or forestry. Although the more desolate open moors and upland areas may appear 'natural', invariably some form of human land use has been and still is being made of them.

To a greater or lesser degree, the contemporary pattern of settlement is dispersed in all areas of rural Britain. In the upland areas, particularly in the Celtic west and north, this is traditional. The nucleated village settlements which now exist in these areas are often relatively recent, frequently dating only from the last century. Many grew around a small industrial enterprise, such as a mine, quarry, factory or minor port, or at the focus of some social or economic activity, such as a church or chapel, a school, a craftsman's workshop, a railway station, or a small market (Fig. 3).

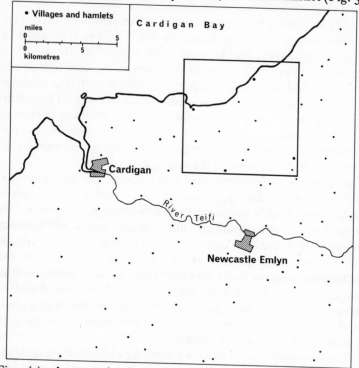

Fig. 3(a)   An example of a dispersed rural settlement pattern in West Wales. See Fig. 3(b) for the boxed area.

By contrast, over much of lowland England, where the normal

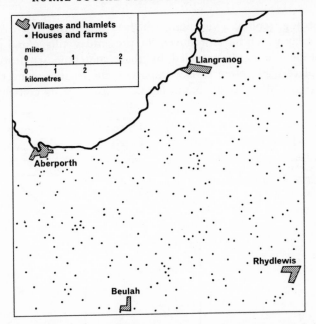

Fig. 3(b) An example of a dispersed rural settlement pattern in West Wales, detail from Fig. 3(a)

pattern has traditionally been that of nucleated villages, an increasingly dispersed local settlement pattern has developed since the enclosures of open fields in the Tudor period (Fig. 4). In many areas, this dispersal accelerated during and after the land enclosure movement in the late eighteenth century as farmsteads, and more recently other dwellings, have been built away from the villages; but to quote Thorpe 'in general the old nuclei still remain remarkably stable features of the rural landscape today'.[1]

Most of Britain's rural population now lives in some form of nucleated settlement. It is immediately apparent, even to a casual observer, that these are of infinite variety in terms of the characteristics of their sites, in their sizes, shapes and functions. However, the morphology of a village and its surrounding area is rarely static. The changes which have occurred within it, and which are still

37

proceeding, require a viewpoint which is long-term. The overlay on overlay which have produced the presentday village and rural landscape are partly revealed by their contemporary features. The place-name often reveals important information concerning the origins of a village. Some facets, at least, of its consequent

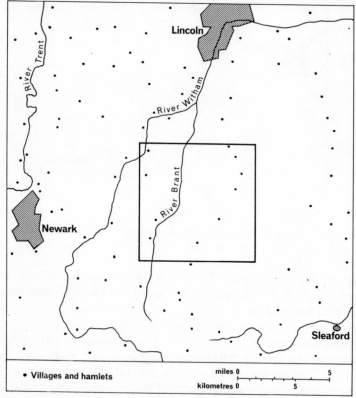

Fig. 4(a)   An example of a nucleated rural settlement pattern in Eastern England. See Fig 4(b) for the boxed area.

development are likely to be divulged by older buildings and streets which are still extant, particularly by the church and the older houses and farmsteadings. Its presentday life is indicated to a considerable extent by the functions of the buildings it contains (and an awareness of those which are absent), while the nature of some of the changes which are occurring is reflected by demolitions, reconstructions, and new building works. The continuity of settlement, of tradition and of social activity are essential ingredients to an understanding of village and rural life.

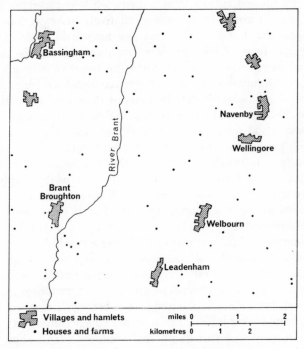

Fig. 4(b) An example of a nucleated rural settlement pattern in Eastern England, detail from Fig. 4(a)

Even though today's population is increasingly mobile and open to outside influences, those social elements which reflect continuity are still likely to have real meaning and a crucial bearing on the inhabitants' reactions to change, or towards proposals for change such as arise, for example, from planning decisions.

AGRICULTURAL AND RURAL FAMILIES

In a hierarchy of *social* units, the basic grouping is the family, followed by the neighbourhood and the community. Today, British rural families are in many respects little different from their urban counterparts. They tend to be relatively small in size, nuclear, with many kinds of decisions being taken more or less jointly by the individuals within them, while connections with a wider kinship group have become relatively loose, at least on a day-to-day basis. Essentially they are household units. This is particularly true for households whose members are not directly involved in agriculture, which form the majority in many rural localities. Occupation, income, reference and friendship groups have become important determinants of their level of living and style of life, but social background and their adherence to certain local norms and roles are still normally of more significance than in urban areas. Work and home are often separate, though not as frequently as in towns and cities, so that differences occur in the daily contacts and experiences of each member of the family.

Although the agricultural population may form only around 2 per cent of our total population, and less than 10 per cent in many administrative counties, in any grouping of rural parishes the proportion often amounts to well over a third of the locality's population. Agricultural families thus frequently form the dominant sector in a rural community. For these families, who are completely or mainly dependent directly on agriculture for their livelihood, little if any separation occurs between home and work.

The farm worker is likely to live in the village (often in a council house) or in a tied cottage on his employer's land. The latter arrangement often has the advantage of a relatively low rent, but the disadvantage of an uncertain security of tenure if the worker loses or changes his job. The relatively low earnings of farm workers have meant that, at least in the past, they have formed the poorest category within a rural community. This situation is slowly changing as fewer workers are being employed on the land. Those who remain have more responsibilities and require greater skills than in the past, and thus more and more frequently earn premiums over the statutory minimum wage; for example, it is not uncommon for a specialised dairyman to feed, milk and care for the health of eighty cows or more, being thus responsible for well over £25,000 of his employer's capital and a substantial part of the farmer's income. The advantages of the agricultural work as perceived by many farm workers (though for others they may appear as disadvantages) include its variety, within each day as well as seasonally, and its nearness to home.

However, the increasing likelihood of neighbours in the village who earn considerably more from non-agricultural employment, often for shorter working hours, with a noticeably 'better' level of living, can and does lead to feelings of dissatisfaction and of relative deprivation among farm workers. Such differences are most apparent near to larger towns and cities, or in other areas where employment opportunities are numerous, despite the earnings of farm workers in such areas often being significantly higher than elsewhere. This encourages further movement out of agriculture.

Some farm workers, especially those who are more traditionally-oriented, may operate small farms on a part-time basis in order to supplement their earnings; others do so as a first step in their aspiration to become farmers. Part-time farming, which has traditionally been customary over much of rural Britain (including, among others, for the clergyman, the publican and the village craftsman), is a persistent and adaptable phenomenon. Although no accurate data are available, it appears to be on the increase in many areas. Farmers, whose acreages and intensity of production are inadequate to assure a sufficient livelihood for their families under current economic conditions, are also taking up non-farming employment while retaining their farm holding on a part-time basis.

In the marginal region between part-time and full-time farming, the integration of farming with other sources of income and the activities they imply for the family is often complex. When the husband on a small farm has a full-time non-agricultural job, much of the work and responsibility for the farm necessarily falls on his

wife and children. Conversely, on a small farm in the sole occupation of the husband, the wife and children commonly supplement
the household income from other work (depending on their
perceived need for additional earnings, their abilities, and the local
availability of employment opportunities).

A major social feature of contemporary British agriculture is
that family farming predominates. Various definitions have been
suggested for a 'family farm', but most would agree that it is one
in which the farm holding provides the main source of livelihood
for the household, with the farm family forming the greater part
of the necessary labour. Precise data on the numbers of holdings
conforming to these criteria are not available. The available evidence
on the sharp decline since 1950 in the numbers of non-family,
hired farm workers suggests that the greater part of the agricultural
labour force in England and Wales is now provided by the farmer
and his family. A medium-sized farm of around 250 acres, which in
the 1930s might have employed six or seven full-time workers in
addition to the farmer and his family, is today commonly operated
by the farmer, assisted by his wife and possibly a son, and one or
at most two hired men. Moreover, during this century farms have
become increasingly owned by their occupiers, which strengthens a
family's bonds with its holding. Around the turn of the century
only about one farm in ten was owner-occupied; today the
proportion is over 60 per cent.

Only a minority of farm holdings are now sufficiently large-
scale businesses to employ a number of workers, given the
prevailing level of technology. These represent the opposite pole
to the small part-time farm holdings. They are of major significance
in the British agricultural economy: the greater part of the
agricultural output is derived from a minority of larger farmers;
some 8 per cent of the holdings in England and Wales, which
employ five or more adult men account for 60 per cent of the
adult male labour force (Table 6). But the significance of these
larger businesses in relation to the social life of rural communities
should not be overemphasised. They are important as sources
of employment, but their owners rarely occupy an equivalent

TABLE 6

Distribution of farm holdings by size and numbers of whole-time adult male workers (including farmers' sons) in England and Wales, 1969

A. Number of holdings

Farm size (acres crops and grass)	Number of whole-time male workers employed, aged 20 – 64						TOTAL	%
	0	1	2	3 or 4	5 – 9	10 and over		
under 50	111,844	9,663	2,356	1,254	522	221	125,850	51.1
50 to 99.75	33,679	10,797	2,211	699	201	65	47,652	19.4
100 to 149.75	12,531	9,066	3,079	903	191	59	25,829	10.5
150 to 299.75	7,383	10,296	7,468	4,090	911	147	30,295	12.3
300 and over	829	1,791	2,998	5,089	4,236	1,631	16,574	6.7
TOTAL	166,266	41,613	18,112	12,035	6,061	2,123	246,210	100.0
%	67.5	16.9	7.4	4.8	2.5	0.9		100.0

B. Number of whole-time adult male workers

Farm size (acres crops and grass)	Number of whole-time male workers employed, aged 20 – 64						TOTAL	%
	0	1	2	3 or 4	5 – 9	10 and over		
under 50	–	9,663	4,712	4,200	3,296	3,994	25,865	13.3
50 to 99.75	–	10,797	4,422	2,307	1,249	1,365	20,140	10.4
100 to 149.75	–	9,066	6,158	2,905	1,131	1,074	20,334	10.5
150 to 299.75	–	10,296	14,936	13,334	5,436	2,522	46,524	24.0
300 and over	–	1,791	5,996	17,467	27,046	28,852	81,152	41.8
TOTAL	–	41,613	36,224	40,213	38,158	37,807	194,015	100.0
%	–	21.4	18.7	20.7	19.7	19.5		100.0

Based on Ministry of Agriculture, Fisheries and Food data

local status to that once held by the 'lord of the manor' or a village squire. In most areas the agricultural ethos of a locality, the social norms and values involved in farm life, are maintained by the majority of farmers, who are invariably family farmers. In the west and upland areas of England and Wales family farms undoubtedly form the overwhelming majority, and they are common in all areas (Fig. 5). However, especially as a consequence

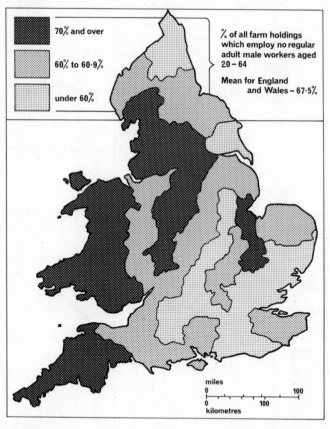

Fig. 5 Proportions of farm holdings employing no regular adult male workers, England and Wales, 1969

of agricultural policy since the mid 1950s, which has stimulated continuous increases in the productivity of farms and the technical efficiency of agricultural production, the family farm of today is invariably business-oriented.

But the family farm also still retains strong elements of what may be termed a 'way of life'. Although this has adapted itself to contemporary society, and is somewhat remote from a *Gemeinschaft*-like system, it subtly affects the social nature of rural communities. This is still apparent, for example, in the importance given to the inheritance and transference of farm property, and the incidence and forms of cooperation among farmers. In both cases, arrangements of a *Gesellschaft*-type, involving legal partnerships between father and son, or contractual arrangements for the joint use by several farmers of machinery (machinery syndicates) or for the bulk purchase of farm requirements by a group of farmers, are increasingly common. But actions in these respects among most farmers are still based largely on custom and informal arrangements.

Traditionally, several customary forms of bequeathing land have existed in Britain, varying in different parts of the country, from inheritance by the eldest son, to equal inheritance among all children, to inheritance by the youngest son. Elements of all these systems still remain, although it is only in recent times, with the growth of owner-occupation, that they have become relevant to the majority of farmers. In the past, in many areas up to the late 1930s, landowning families expanded or contracted their estates, by investment or marriage, often with little regard for their tenant farmers. Among smaller landowners, the equivalent of presentday owner-occupier family farmers, 'successful' marriages of the children led to a growing number of acres being owned by the family, and increasingly complex networks within the extended family involving numerous reciprocal arrangements of sharing and cooperation.

Farm inheritance today has become a more widespread issue, and a problem. The economic pressures on farming are such that the splitting of a farm among several sons, particularly if it is in the medium-size range, is recognised by farmers as a regressive step, although instances still occur. Setting up one or more sons (and maybe daughters and their husbands) in farming is still a social norm which is given a high priority among family farmers in many areas. In part, the problems are solved by increasing numbers of farm children who, largely as a result of their education, do not wish to succeed to the family farm. Where one or more sons have wished to remain in farming, the recent solution has often been for them to have been taken into legal partnership with their father.

This latter adaptation to modern conditions is in many senses a *de jure* recognition of the joint intrafamily decision-making which is characteristic of most family farms. Instances still occur where one or more sons, even in middle age, are in effect working on their home farm as hired workers, but this has progressively become less common. Rapidly changing agricultural technology and the need to incorporate business management procedures have generally meant a degree of specialisation and division of labour within the farm family. Even on rented farms, where security of tenure to the occupier has been assured since 1947 (though not necessarily to his son as a successor), the joint father-son(s) management of the holding has frequently been similarly formalised.

Interfarm cooperation similarly exhibits trends toward more *Gesellschaft*-like forms. In many respects, the need to cooperate is less than in the past, since high levels of farm mechanisation mean that most farms can themselves cope with many tasks which in the past required a great deal of labour for short periods, a problem solved by cooperation among neighbours. However, for certain specialised or new operations, the current tendencies are towards more formal contractual modes of cooperation, although a variety of informal, cooperative activities still commonly exist among farmers in most areas. The Central Council for Agricultural and Horticultural Cooperation, established under the 1967 Agriculture Act, fosters newer forms of joint action among farmers. It should also be noted that nowadays cooperating farmers are not necessarily adjacent farmers; the groups often consist of members widely dispersed over a rural community.

In terms of the farming population, the networks of interaction within rural communities are usually well developed. Farmers, farm workers and their families are likely to be as involved as anyone in the general social organisations in a rural area, including activities which occur in accessible urban centres. In addition, some organisations which are apparently specific to the farming population are open to others; for example, Young Farmers' Clubs are notable in providing what is often the only form of youth club in rural areas. Farm families, however, are also normally involved in several organisations and activities which are specifically agricultural. Increasingly, in addition to membership of farmers' unions and trading agricultural cooperatives, farmers are participating in various formal groupings and joint activites, for example, for bulk buying or group selling under contract, or in discussion groups. As in all more formal groups, leadership is vital, but it is rare that this is lacking among farmers; the intense interest and activity of one person or a minority of members usually explains a group's origin, function and membership. Outside support is also generally important, and this is available for a variety of purposes from the professional agricultural advisers of the Ministry of Agriculture, Fisheries and Food, or of the three Agricultural Colleges in Scotland.

From the point of view of farmers, their families and others less directly involved, all such groups and organisations offer means for profitable interaction, entered into voluntarily. Further, they affect the wider networks of interrelationships among farmers and other rural dwellers through other associations which members maintain outside any particular group. It is the perpetuation of such meaningful relationships within a rural community (which is recognisable as such and meaningful to an individual) which sustain communities as social realities.

The farm family thus shows itself to be adaptable to the modern economic, social and technological environment. The fulltime farm family remains as the rural family in its most typical form, while the family situation of part-time farmers and of farm workers approaches it at several points. Moreover, the farm family, more than most in contemporary society, is usually a 'stem family'; more authoritarian, patriarchal forms are now rare. It not only can but does provide economic as well as social and psychological support for its members at the homestead, while through its network of personal relationships within the rural community it provides ample social experience and flexibility. It is implicit in the context of presentday agricultural conditions and of educational opportunities that the farm family is permissive towards the mobility of some or all of its children, both socially and geographically. The smaller the family farm business, the greater the tendency and need for its children to seek other employment.

As the typical form of social organisation in British agriculture, the prime characteristics of full-time family farms are that they not only manage a commercial business at which they live, but also take most of the decisions regarding the farm and its operation as a family, own most or all of the capital involved, and provide most or all of the labour required. To a large degree this both reflects and sustains the well-known value of independence associated with family farming. But this independence is strictly limited and refers primarily to some economic aspects of the farming enterprise. In several economic and most social activities various interdependencies and relationships exist which stretch beyond the farm and even beyond the village or local neighbourhood (Fig. 6).

VILLAGE AND NEIGHBOURHOOD

Up to this point, three terms have been used more or less synonymously, namely, a 'village', a 'rural community' and a 'rural locality'. The term 'community' is used in various ways even among social scientists, to the extent that its meaning has often become value-loaded or emotive or both. Even so, there is much to be said for its retention in discussing rural society. Villages and their

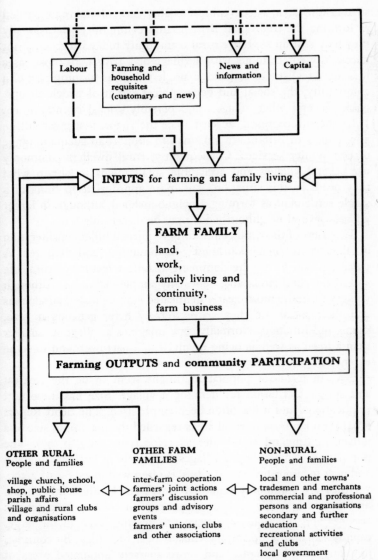

Fig. 6   The family farm as a focus of rural social relationships

surrounding area, a geographical locality, have often been regarded as forming the traditional British rural community. Occasionally they may still do so, but a rural community today is certainly not necessarily coterminous with a village or a parish. In most cases it is more realistic to consider a single village as forming part of a community, the social and geographical extent of which encompasses several other villages, and possibly a local country town. It has been recognised, at least since the 1930s, that most village populations in Britain are too small to support an adequate range of community services. Consequently, rural dwellers commonly use several villages and accessible small towns to obtain what they need. In this situation, it is more appropriate to think of a single settlement as forming a neighbourhood, although in larger villages several neighbourhoods may be discernible.

This view of the rural community requires a fuller consideration of the terms 'neighbourhood', 'community' and 'village'. A *village*, which forms the dominant, manifest feature of rural life and of the rural landscape, defies any simple definition. Although villages form the most clearly delineated expressions of rural areas and their social life they are extremely heterogeneous in size, shape and function. Normally, one imagines a village as smaller than a town as well as being involved in a narrower, and to some extent different spectrum of functions.

Size, in terms of population, might seem to be the clearest and simplest criterion for defining a village. Size has important implications, and it has often been emphasised. The Scott Report (1942)[2] on land use in rural areas regarded the maximum size of a village in England and Wales as 1,500 (para. 196, p. 67). The population of many larger villages, especially in lowland England and near to larger towns and cities, is often well in excess of 2,500, yet they are commonly regarded as villages by their inhabitants and are recognisably such to a visitor. Many of the characteristic services and functions of a town are missing, even in the large, rapidly expanding dormitory villages near the cities. By contrast, in many of the remoter and more sparsely populated areas of Britain, the larger villages may perform the functions usually associated with a town, serving a wide area. Table 7 indicates the size distribution of rural parishes in Great Britain, and in three contrasting counties.

It is often easier, and more meaningful to distinguish a lower rather than an upper size limit for a village. Thorpe[1] defined a British village as a 'nucleated rural settlement of twenty or more homesteads, a large village being distinguishable from a small market town by its paucity of services' (p. 359), with smaller settlements being regarded as 'hamlets'. Recent studies in north-east England have indicated that settlements with under about ninety adults (say forty to fifty households) must be regarded as hamlets since they lack even the minimum services expected in a small village—the school has probably been closed, there may be no shop, and the bus service is inadequate.[3] However, the number of villages or hamlets lacking the basic services of a piped water supply and electricity are now rare.

In parenthesis, one should state that everywhere that is called 'a village' is not the rural settlement with which we are concerned. Clearly, the old villages which have been engulfed by urban growth but which still retain the word in their name (at least as used locally) are in no sense rural, although their inhabitants may express strong neighbourhood differences between themselves and adjacent suburbs. Again, some recent attempts to create 'new villages', set in a rural landscape but which in reality are urban suburbs physically detached from a town or city, are unlikely to be villages in the rural sense; their artificiality may in time give way to the growth of village characteristics, although these are unlikely to be fostered by a highly mobile, completely middle-class population. Despite many problems, particularly those involving social cohesion, the addition of new housing estates to older, middle-sized villages is more likely, in time, to lead to a perpetuation of village life.

The definitions of, and distinctions between, a *neighbourhood* consisting of several families or households, and a *community*, also present problems. At best, the margin between them must be somewhat arbitrary, and its determination will certainly differ

51

TABLE 7
Size distribution of 'rural parishes'* in Great Britain, 1961

Total population of 'parishes'	GREAT BRITAIN No. of 'parishes'	%	CARDIGANSHIRE No. of 'parishes'	%	LEICESTERSHIRE No. of 'parishes'	%	SURREY No. of 'parishes'	%
0 – 499	6775	57.2	48	66.7	124	57.1	8	11.6
500 – 999	2232	18.8	18	25.0	41	18.9	17	24.6
1000 – 1999	1539	13.0	5	6.9	20	9.2	12	17.4
2000 – 2999	553	4.7	1	1.4	11	5.1	13	18.8
3000 – 3999	295	2.5	–	–	8	3.7	8	11.6
4000 – 4999	143	1.2	–	–	6	2.8	1	1.5
5000 and over	306	2.6	–	–	7	3.2	10	14.5
Mean 'parish' population	909		492		1,032		2,573	
Median size group of 'parishes'	400 – 499		300 – 399		300 – 399		1000 – 1999	
% of total population in 'rural' districts	21.0		66.0		32.8		10.3	

* 'Rural parishes' include all civil parishes in rural districts in England and Wales, and county council electoral divisions in Scotland.

over time and regionally. Both depend on various linkages between individuals and families, but in a developed rural society the community is the lowest-order social groupings which approaches a self-sufficiency in the daily social needs of its inhabitants, where those who live in it are consciously aware of their inter-dependence.

Social interaction may be expected to be at its most intense, outside the family, at the neighbourhood level. But, to a large extent, the effective neighbourhood is individually determined; all one's physically adjacent neighbours may not be included in the group one actually recognises as 'neighbours'. This is often clear, for example, in the groups of farmers who informally cooperate with each other in various farming activities.[4] The neighbourhood in a rural area is invariably significant sociologically since it indicates various connections between individuals and families of a more intense form than is possible at the community level. As microcosmic groupings, which will frequently correspond to friendship groups, peer groups, cliques and reference groups, they form the essential bridge between the individual person and family, and the local community. In comparison with the community, a neighbourhood is less than self-sufficient, although this is not to imply that a self-sufficiency exists in every respect at the community level; the emphasis is on the satisfaction of people's needs in terms of services and organisations.

Hillery, in a notable review of the literature on 'the community', was able to discover ninety-four definitions which were sufficiently different to be considered distinct.[5] He concluded that: 'A majority of the definitions include the following as important elements of the community: area, common ties, and social interaction (in increasing importance for each separate element respectively)' (p. 118). In addition, several secondary criteria may be more or less important in differing situations (see Table 8). Although it is difficult to specify precise quantities for many of these criteria, it is useful (especially in the rural context) to consider the limits of a community as occurring where there is an optimal combination between social interaction and recognised

TABLE 8
Criteria which have been used to define a community

Primary criteria:	Geographical area		Social interaction emphasising Common Ties, and
		or	A common characteristic other than area
Secondary criteria:	Self-sufficiency. Common life (although a community is always part of a larger society). Consciousness among members of belonging. Possession of common values and norms. Collection of accessible institutions and organisations. Locality groups.		

common ties among people on the one hand, and the area within which they are able to satisfy most of their daily recurrent social needs on the other; communication and interdependence are at the core of the concept of a community. As area expands outwards from the household to the village, the parish and beyond, and the number of people included consequently rises, there is an increasing likelihood that people's needs for work, shopping, education, religion, recreation, and other services can be satisfied. But there will also be a tendency for a smaller proportion of people to know each other, to have progressively weaker ties with each other, and to matter less to each other. Beyond a certain limit one is in a different, adjacent community. Clearly, the community cannot be regarded as a static phenomenon. Changes or improvements in the means of communication and travelling, and alterations in the organisation of various institutions (e.g. retailing, education and religion), usually mean that the area covered by a rural community is tending to grow.

There is thus a degree of correspondence, although it is less than perfect, between social groupings and the type of settlement. The family, as a result of its tendency to become smaller in size and more nuclear in character, can progressively be equated more with the household. This is also true even among those farm families whose mobility is relatively low and whose kinship connections within a rural area still matter. Neighbourhoods may correspond to any situation within a range stretching from a small collection of households in close proximity to the whole of a hamlet, or a small village, or even a relatively large village together with a surrounding area, its scale and character depending particularly on the presence of individuals or families who perform specific roles and functions. Finally, rural communities appear to be expanding in area with their boundaries becoming less distinct, including numerous villages and other settlements within the service areas of several, adjacent country towns; and thus the community partially contains such country towns within it.

Rural social structure and organisation
II. The rural community

As a first approximation, a rural *community* may be regarded as the population living within the sphere of influence and service or the catchment area, of a 'central place'—a larger village or country town—upon which the people are largely dependent It is only at such a centre that a range of wellstocked shops supermarkets, bank branches, the offices of commercial and service organisations, and services such as secondary schools health centres and hospitals, can be viably maintained. These together with the presence of a range of tradesmen (builders plumbers, electricians, etc.), whose services are available in the surrounding rural area, and the existence of a variety of usually small-scale industries, imply that such places are also employment centres.

During this century, and especially since the 1920s as motor vehicles have become commonly available, and as local and central government and other agencies have placed their offices and service points in selected centres, the effective community area has tended to expand, with economic and social provisions being increasingly concentrated in the larger settlements. This has been a case of action and reaction initiated and maintained both as a result of the willingness and ability of rural dwellers to travel more often to local towns to obtain certain services, as well as the tendency of national, regional and county organisations to withdraw their offices from smaller settlements. This has meant that many villages, often including larger villages, have become denuded of many functions which they possessed in the early part of this century. The range of services they had to maintain was necessarily

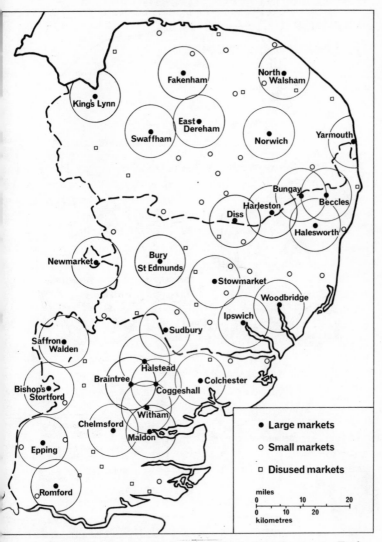

Fig. 7 Markets in East Anglia in the early nineteenth century. Each large market has an arbitrary six mile market radius. (1. Large markets 2. Small markets 3. Disused or declining markets)

57

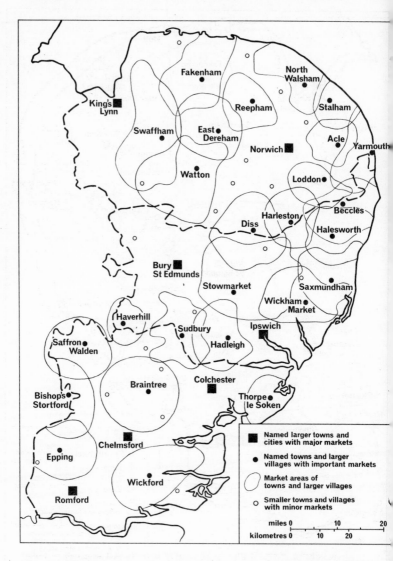

Fig. 8 Market areas in East Anglia in 1931 (excluding those of larger towns and cities, and of villages with minor markets)

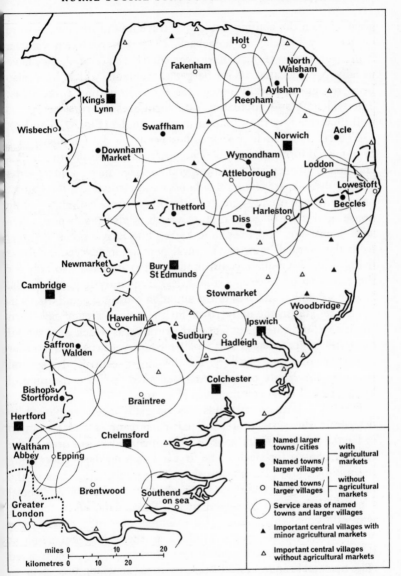

Fig. 9 Service areas of East Anglian county towns and larger villages in 1971

greater when the common modes of travelling in rural areas were on foot, by bicycle, on horseback, or in a horsedrawn vehicle. Moreover, as new services have evolved, or been created, they have usually been located in the larger settlements which have also been recognised locally as centres for surrounding rural areas. The widening and fluctuating catchment areas of rural centres is well illustrated by the situation in East Anglia (Figs. 7, 8 and 9).

The result of such processes has been the development, in a pronounced form, of a complex hierarchy of centres, from hamlets and small villages at the lower end to large metropolitan areas at the other. Apart from a few houses and farmsteads, the hamlet or small village usually contains little other than a church, a public house, and a small general store which is also a sub-post office with a post-box and telephone kiosk. The larger urban centres, from the point of view of the rural population (except for those living in the immediately surrounding area) are looked to only for the provision of more specialised, less frequently required needs. Bracey's detailed analyses of the situation during the mid-1940s in Wiltshire[2] and in the early 1950s for the central area of Southern England[3], [4] indicate the extent of the rural areas which were served by many larger villages and smaller country towns (lower-order district centres), as well as by the larger centres. In several respects, the limits of the areas delimited indicate meaningful boundaries of rural communities (Fig. 10).

One of two main methods has normally been employed to determine the service area of particular centres and to rank in order the relative importance of those included in any area of the country chosen for study. The first is based on data concerning the number, and possibly the sizes (for example, in terms of the numbers of workers employed at each) of the economic and social functions contained in a settlement. These data, often together with additional information (for example, on traffic flows in the area), reflect the provisions available to the population living at the centre and in a surrounding area. Recently more sophisticated statistical techniques have been used to analyse such data to produce a more precise ranking of places and their spheres of

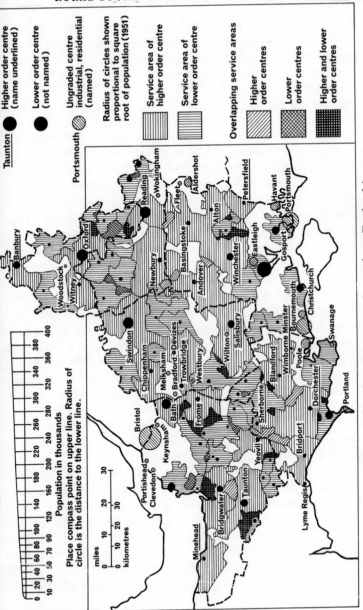

Fig. 10 Rural service centres in southern England in 1953

influence (see, for example, Rowley, 1970).[5] This method, however, tends to view the population in a rural area as dependent on one particular central place for its needs, but without much direct evidence that the inhabitants in the area defined make such use of the place.

The second method is based on asking rural dwellers which centres they actually use for various purposes. This has the advantage of separating the rural from the urban component in the provisions at a given centre in terms of both their availability and use. This was the method used by Bracey in assigning a score for the 'rural component of centrality' to settlements in southern England, and distinguishing between higher and lower-order district centres (Fig. 11). As he notes (ref. 4, p. 41), it is also a method which 'takes notice of the fact that in certain areas, particularly those transitional to a service territory, more than one centre may be visited for different services or, indeed, the same service'. In recent years, this overlapping in the service areas of various places appears to have become, and is still becoming, an increasingly dominant phenomenon as a result of the growing mobility of the rural population and the resulting lowering of their allegiance to one particular centre and the services available there. It is only in the rural area immediately surrounding a large town or city that such a centre may be used almost exclusively, and even so various conditions may result in uses being made of other, more distant, even smaller centres. For example, a city located at a county boundary may mean that rural inhabitants who use it for most purposes have to use another centre for local government services.

The overlapping in the use of several centres by the rural population is most clearly seen away from the immediate vicinity of the larger towns and cities, but in areas where market towns and larger villages are rarely more than eight to ten miles apart. This is the common situation over much of England. If one seeks to define a rural community in terms of the territory served by a particular central place the result is necessarily imprecise. It is only in the less densely populated upland areas of Wales, the north of England and much of Scotland, where towns are fewer and further apart, that more or less discrete service territories

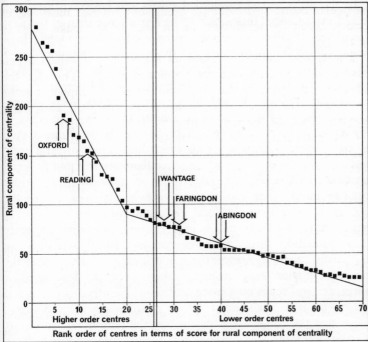

Fig. 11   Centrality of rural service centres in southern England in 1953

survive. In these situations, a degree of correspondence still exists between rural communities and the town service areas. In most cases, however, apart from the uses made by rural people of their local towns and their attachments to them, there is also the overlay of influence and service provision by more distant, larger towns and cities. As higher-order service centres, these may be used for employment by only a small minority of the rural people, and be visited only occasionally for purchasing requirements, but these centres often exert a continuous influence over a wide rural area in terms of local government, administration and major public service, or as the places where local newspapers are published.

In the areas served by market towns and larger villages, one would expect social interaction to be less intense than in the past when the effective community corresponded more closely to a single village. The basis for and existence of a community based on social relationships, therefore, might appear to be weaker and less real. However, it is maintained to a considerable degree by the participation of rural inhabitants in various social organisations, within villages and in neighbouring towns. The effect of the larger territory and population numbers is also counteracted by the increased frequency with which individuals in rural areas can and do visit one or more larger settlements and join in social activities, by the easier contacts which are possible over a wider rural area and by knowledge of activities in that area, and by the use of the telephone, the local Press and other media. Near to large towns and cities this is progressively more difficult, since the dominating forms of economic and social activities are essentially urban. However, there is evidence to suggest that the rural population may strongly retain or even develop their allegiance and focus on a more traditional country town which is peripheral to a city's direct sphere of influence. This does not mean that the city is avoided, but that the peripheral centres are viewed as more meaningful for many rural-oriented social activities. For example, in the East Midlands, where the cities of Nottingham, Leicester and Derby dominate the surrounding countryside, several thriving country towns continue as the recognised centres of rural communities (such as Newark, Melton Mowbray, Market Harborough and Ashby-de-la-Zouch).

The kinds of social activities and organisations which exist and flourish in rural areas, and the general structure of such social organisations, not only exemplify but also reinforce the importance of the villages and local country towns in maintaining a meaningful rural community. This is not the place to enter into a detailed description of rural organisations; for a detailed account, which is by no means out of date, see Bracey (1959).[6] Even at the level of a very small village, some organised social activity invariably exists, usually centred on the church or the public house. Such villages and their parishes are often too small to have a parish council, but the required annual parish meeting is often a real forum for the organised discussion of the neighbourhood's problems and needs. In larger villages and country towns, where convenient meeting places are likely to be available (such as a village hall, or a church hall, or a school room), a variety of organisations often flourish.

To a very large extent the initiation, success and survival of any organised social activity depends on the leadership available and the interest and support of the relevant people. This is nowhere clearer than in rural communities where the potential membership for any organisation, especially at a neighbourhood level, is relatively small, and where the actual membership is often low. Yet thriving organisations often exist with under twenty members. This situation is often easier to maintain where the aims of a club or meeting are well defined, and are supported by a wider movement to which it is attached (either a county or regional association of the same kind of organisation, or a national organisation). This usually means a degree of interaction, usually friendly rivalry and cooperation, and the social relationships thus evolved with similar groups in neighbouring areas, together with encouragement from a central body. Such connections regularly occur in various rural organisations, including the churches and chapels, the Young Farmers' Clubs and other youth clubs, the Women's Institutes, and the farmers' unions and various farmers' discussion groups. Whether the area from which members and supporters are drawn is very local or a wider territory depends on the geographical distribution of various organised activities which in turn results from contemporary initiative and leadership, as well as a continuing tradition.

In all cases, organisations change and react to the needs and allegiances of the people they serve. On the whole, as in the case of economic and social services, the tendency is for rural organisations to serve progressively larger areas, although the location of meetings and other activities is not necessarily always concentrated in the larger villages and country towns. In part, also, this arises from various forms of reorganisation becoming common in recent years. For example, two or more rural parishes and their churches being united or formed into a 'plurality' under one vicar, or a 'circuit' of rural chapels being served by one minister, or the closure of many smaller primary schools with a concentration on one particular village school, has often meant an organisational base which is greater than one village or parish. But the area and population involved is still much less than that served by a local market town or that which comprises a rural community.

Several services which people use are located in centres which are decreed by various authorities. For example, children in certain parishes normally have to attend the secondary school located in a particular large village or town; or people have to use the offices of certain local and central government services located in particular places. But these only partially determine people's movements and contacts with each other. Most social interaction, participation in organised activities, and use of various services at central places is based on free choice. To a large extent rural dwellers today choose the area, place and circumstances where they meet other people, and thus with which people they associate. The rural community as it actually exists is thus the result of the complex networks of movements and more or less intimate knowledge of other people arising from their associations and social activities.

It was emphasised earlier that in many of the villages and parishes for which 'community studies' are available, the relative positions of individuals and families is more a matter of behaviour (status role) than of the application of socio-economic criteria (social class). To a large degree, although of necessity not as completely as at a village level (which is likely to consist of only one or two neighbourhoods), this still persists at the rural community level. Social interaction implies that social positions are recognised and individuals' actions noticed in ways which matter to themselves and to their families, friends and acquaintances.

Occupation, income, wealth and evidence of conspicuous consumption become more important as criteria by which people assess and differentiate each other as the area and size of the population increases, but a meaningful community is not so large that account is not taken of people's skills, religious and other organisational attachments, recreational activities and abilities, and still, almost invariably in the rural context, of a person's origin and background. Frequently the evaluations made of individuals and of their kin and associates in the past (even an apparently remote past) as well as in recent times remain effective in judging and determining present social positions. Despite the growing presence of new residents in many rural areas, a relatively high degree of interpersonal knowledge and communication is possible and can be maintained in the rural community. To the extent that 'newcomers' can be and are assessed by the normal criteria, their integration into the community is enhanced.

AN EXAMPLE: NORTH-WEST BERKSHIRE

No two areas of the country are identical, but many of the general observations which have been made concerning the contemporary nature of a rural community in Britain may be exemplified by a more detailed, though necessarily brief, consideration of one area.

The landscape of north-west Berkshire, between Wantage and Faringdon, is immediately recognisable as rural to the casual observer. It is also an area of considerable natural beauty, with the River Thames forming its northern boundary. Immediately south, parallel to the river, is a rich, arable farming area on a low ridge, along which are sited several villages within a mile or two of each other. The centre and larger part of the area consists of the low-lying Vale of the White Horse, the villages and hamlets being located on slight elevations. Here, livestock husbandry, mainly dairy farming, is predominant. To the south are the Berkshire Downs, with a line of villages along the edge of the Vale, with the parishes stretching from the summit of the Downs, where arable farming with sheep is general, over the steep north face, into the Vale.

As elsewhere in rural Britain, the present social situation (summer 1971) is not static. Changes which arise from national policy, such as the impending reorganisation of the structure of local government, will undoubtedly affect the local administration and location of many public services. The effect of planning policy, which is increasingly taking into account the views and opinions of local residents, will affect the location and pace of future developments. However, many existing patterns are well-established and resilient, and forces which stimulate change will affect them more slowly.

The area lies on the periphery of the south-east region of England. So far, it is beyond the range of commuting into London as well as of most of the direct influences of the metropolis. Similarly, it is somewhat remote from the regional capitals of adjacent regions, Bristol to the south-west and Birmingham to the north. However, as is usual over most of England, the rural area we shall consider is within easy access of several large towns or cities (Fig. 12). Oxford to the north-east and Swindon to the south-west are relatively near, and these, together with Reading, some twenty-five miles to the east, provide the area with centres for employment, shopping, recreational and other social activities, and with commercial and professional services. In addition, nearby on the east lie Abingdon, a traditional market town with industrial development; Didcot, a large, rapidly expanding industrial village; and Harwell with its Atomic Energy Research Establishment.

Traditionally, as today, the daily recurring market, commercial and professional needs of the area have been served mainly by the small town of Wantage in the west, around which a considerable population expansion is planned in the future (a development which has already begun), and the large village of Faringdon (which is locally regarded as a town) in the west. The larger villages of Stanford in the Vale and Uffington have also been important locally as service centres, while recent population

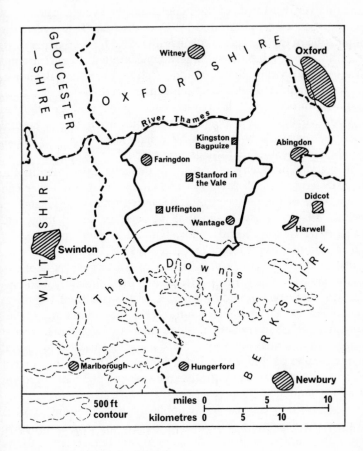

Fig. 12   North-west Berkshire

expansion at Grove (until a few years ago, a small hamlet adjacent to Wantage on the north) and at Kingston Bagpuize has meant the growth of retailing and other services at both. The total population of the area is approximately 30,000, which represents an overall population density of 46 persons per 100 acres (or nearly 300 per square mile). Apart from the two towns and larger villages, which

69

contain over two-thirds of the population, the average number of people per 100 acres is around 17. Over the past twenty years the population in the area as a whole has increased by over 50 per cent, but this growth has been largely concentrated at and around Wantage, Faringdon, Stanford in the Vale and Kingston Bagpuize. In the remainder of the area, population increase has also been common, but at a much lower rate (under 25 per cent growth from 1951 to 1970), with a population decline occurring in several parishes, particularly those which have had relatively small numbers of inhabitants (usually under 200).

A marked hierarchy of village settlements exists within the area, in terms both of their size and character. At the lower end of the scale are purely agricultural hamlets and small villages as well as small, largely 'residential' villages, in which many old cottages have been recently renovated and are now inhabited by urban middle-class workers or retired people. At the other end, but smaller than Wantage and Faringdon, are large villages of two kinds: some are largely rural-oriented and predominantly working-class in character, providing services and agricultural requisites mainly for a restricted surrounding area; and some are predominantly suburban residential estates in a rural setting. In recent years a varying quantity of new housing has been added to several of the smaller as well as the larger villages, although the current planning policy is to concentrate expansion and population growth at and around Wantage.

None of the villages are completely self-sufficient, nor is Wantage or Faringdon. The smaller villages and neighbourhoods, have often undergone considerable reorganisation recently. Many of the smaller village primary schools have been closed. Ecclesiastically, several of the parishes have been united or formed into pluralities. However, most villages still contain one or more public houses and a general store (including a sub-post office within it) while several have a petrol-filling and car-servicing station. A Women's Institute meets once a month in most of the settlements.

In a very real sense, however, this area forms one rural community. It is recognised as such by most of its inhabitants, although the 'newcomers' at Grove and Kingston Bagpuize may be only partially integrated into it so far (and further expansion planned for Grove may even prevent this occurring). Apart from people being frequently employed outside the area, most of the recurring needs of the inhabitants are satisfied by the combined provisions available at Wantage, Faringdon and a few larger villages. Most of the commercial and professional services are concentrated in Wantage and Faringdon, two centres which Bracey[4] distinguished as important lower-order centres in the south of England (Figs. 10 and 11). Of the two, Wantage dominates for shopping and business services, while Faringdon is generally more important for entertainment and recreation. However, there are also several tradesmen and merchants serving the area, who live in and work from one or other of the villages. For example, of the thirty or so villages in the area, seven have one or more builders, three have a baker, and three have agricultural merchants. Two grammar schools serve the area, one in Wantage for boys and the other in Faringdon for girls. In both cases, friendships are created over the area as a whole. The district nurses and health visitors based at the Faringdon Health Centre cover most of the area. Meetings and discussion groups among farmers are held at several points, while some farmers also regularly attend agricultural meetings and events in Oxford, Newbury or Reading, thus making contact with farmers over a wider territory. Two Young Farmers' Clubs serve the area, one at Wantage, whose members are mainly from the immediate neighbourhood, and the Faringdon club, which meets in a small village in the Vale and whose members are drawn not only from over the whole area but also from well beyond. The relatively few Nonconformist chapels means that they usually serve considerably wider areas than the villages in which they are located.

These and other social activities, which result in social relationships being formed and maintained throughout the area, override the effects of certain administrative and other divisions. As at present organised, the area lies in three Rural Districts, the western half in Faringdon R.D., three parishes in the north-east of the area in Abingdon R.D., and the remainder in Wantage R.D. (while Wantage itself is an administratively separate Urban District). Therefore in the rural area inhabitants have to look to different centres for certain local government services. The catchment territories of the non-grammar secondary schools in Faringdon and Wantage also divide the area. Less socially significant divisions also exist in terms of the rural deaneries, the administrative territories of the Church of England, post office deliveries and collections (from Wantage and Faringdon) and two telephone areas (Gloucester in the western half, and Oxford). Daily milk delivery is mainly from either of two large dairies in Grove, covering the eastern part of the area, and in Faringdon, although a small private retailer in Stanford in the Vale also supplies milk in a central part (Fig. 13).

The area as a whole, however, remains one in which most of the inhabitants throughout recognise a variety of common bonds among themselves, certainly a sufficiency of similarities to consider themselves as one rural community. The towns and larger villages, as service centres, largely reinforce and maintain this in ways which foster the integration of the community, the inhabitants having allegiances to several according to their needs, preferences, customary habits or personal idiosyncrasies. The result is a variety of intertwining networks which together produce the fabric of social relationships existing in the rural area.

A SYNTHETIC VIEW

In so far as theories and explanatory models have been used to define and analyse a community, especially a community in the rural environment, these have originated primarily from two sources. Both are relevant in seeking a fuller appreciation of the nature of contemporary rural communities, although they have often remained separate, and their approaches and results have been reconciled only by implication.

Theories used by sociologists and social anthropologists have mainly emphasised patterns of social relationships and allegiances. Investigations derived from these bases have usually started from a micro level of families and kinship, peer and reference groupings, extending outwards to wider, more diffuse networks of relationships. Several of the British 'community studies' indicated earlier have used an approach of this kind, although not necessarily in order to delimit the boundaries of a community. Social geographers, on the other hand, have usually been concerned with the services available at various settlements (central places) and their service areas or spheres of influence. These data have formed the basis for constructing a hierarchy of settlements and service territories. In relatively isolated areas, and particularly in earlier times when the possibilities did not exist for most people to travel regularly

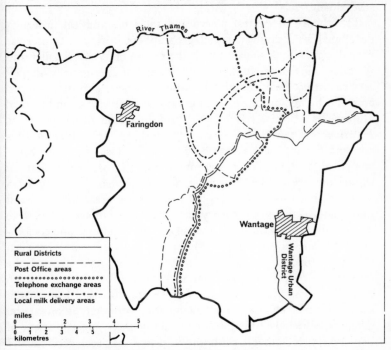

Fig. 13 Service divisions within the Vale of the White Horse, Berkshire, in 1971

over a wide area and the population, especially in rural areas, was generally more stable, a high degree of correspondence often existed between the more or less discrete service area of a market town or larger village and the effective rural community. Over most of contemporary rural Britain, these conditions no longer exist, and the correlation between service areas and social relationships is less real.

From the point of view of a particular large settlement, the service area and its boundaries can still be defined in such a way that the comparable areas of adjacent central places appear more or less discrete. But the actual situation for the rural population *within* such territories, including the inhabitants of lower order settlements, is that they maintain allegiances and attachments to several centres.

The theory of central places and their hierarchical ordering, developed by European social geographers during the interwar period, generally associated with the names of W. Christaller and A. Lösch, involved the heuristic concept of hexagonally-shaped service areas, each contained within a larger, similarly shaped area of a higher-order centre; for various applications and critical evaluations of this, reference should be made to Haggett's is *Locational Analysis in Human Geography*.[7] In applying this concept in empirical research, despite the use of sophisticated analytical techniques in recent years, the determination of significant breaks has created problems. It has generally been assumed that the boundaries between service areas lie in a rural hinterland, although the theory has not required this to be the case. The implication is therefore that significant economic and sociological divisions occur within the rural territory lying between urban centres, although more recent studies have stressed the importance, within rural hinterlands, of the overlapping which exists between the service areas of several towns. As indicated earlier in this chapter, a characteristic, common among rural dwellers, which is functional in creating their consciousness of belonging to a definable community, is that they seek services and interrelate among each other in terms of several central places.

The definition of a rural community purely on the basis of discrete service areas around central places is thus erroneous in that, starting from an urban point of view, it suggests the exclusive dependence of the surrounding rural population on one urban centre. Moreover, the impression is easily created that such an order of things is static. Over time, the activities and reactions resulting from the interrelationships between a rural community and two or more urban centres lead to changes in the provisions available at such centres (especially those which are more rurally and agriculturally oriented, such as markets and agricultural supplies), and thus in the allegiances of rural dwellers. This operates in two ways. In terms of many of the traditional functions, for example, schools or doctors' surgeries, or various tradesmen such as blacksmiths (who have generally transformed themselves into agricultural engineers or machinery repairers), builders, bakers, butchers, etc., the tendency has been for them to become concentrated in fewer larger centres. On the other hand, for several newer functions, such as car-servicing stations or electrical tradesmen, which initially were available only in larger centres, their availability has diffused to smaller settlements, though not necessarily to the very smallest, in response to a growing effective social need. From the point of view of the rural community, the result is to create variable and unstable allegiances to several differing centres.

The traditional pattern (Fig. 14), still extant in the earlier decades of this century, has generally given way to a different pattern. The more diverse and widespread attachments of rural people, based largely on individual choice and preferences, sometimes to their own village, sometimes to another village, and invariably for several of their needs to more than one country town (and possibly to one or more large town or city within twenty to thirty miles), mean that the rural community has become less dependent on the services and influences of any one place (Fig. 15). Despite certain divisions within the geographical area of a rural community prescribed by various administrative authorities, it has become increasingly meaningful socially in

75

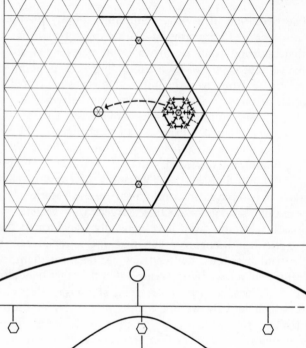

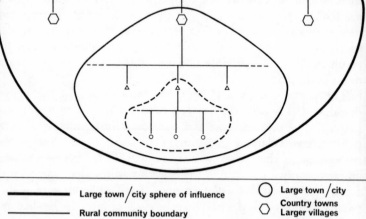

——————— Large town/city sphere of influence	⬡ Large town/city
——————— Rural community boundary	⬡ Country towns Larger villages
– – – – – – – Neighbourhood boundary	△ Villages
	○ Hamlets

Fig. 14   The traditional concept of a rural community based on one country town and within a settlement hierarchy

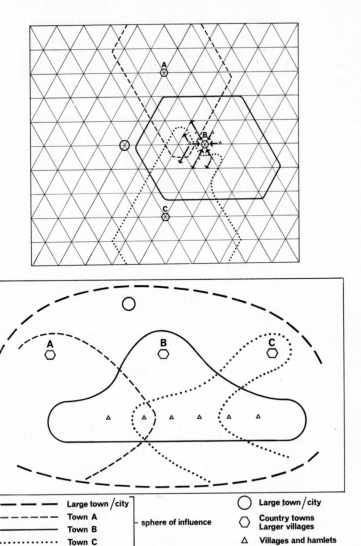

‒ ‒ ‒ ‒ ‒ ‒ Large town/city	⬭ sphere of influence
‒ ‒ ‒ ‒ ‒ Town A	
———— Town B	
············· Town C	

◯ Large town/city

⬡ Country towns
Larger villages

△ Villages and hamlets

Fig. 15 The contemporary rural community

terms of multiplex internal relationships, which are reinforced by the numerous linkages with urban centres. The rural community is thus a continuing institution. Despite its tendency in recent years to increase in size (territorially and in terms of population), thus containing not only more neighbourhoods but various local social groups which are of a socially diffuse nature, the contemporary British rural community in many senses exhibits progressively more self-identification. This results from and illustrates its ability to adapt to the urbanised character of the society as a whole.

Change in contemporary rural society 6

To visualise rural communities and the lives of country people as relatively static and unchanging, in contrast to the dynamic character of urban living, is erroneous, although such a myth is still prevalent. Elements of stability normally exist in an urban as well as a rural environment. Various processes stimulating change also occur throughout society, although the processes are not necessarily operative in identical ways in all sectors.

It is widely believed that the more peasantlike or *Gemeinschaft*-like a social system, the more resistant are the people to accept change. Not only is the normative range of any accepted role or behaviour relatively narrow, but due to this a high degree of conformity exists to the local social norms, while any deviation from them is quickly sanctioned and the deviant is ostracised, or reconforms. Under such a system the introduction of change appears difficult. Yet viewed over a period of time it is surprising how much change has often occurred in peasant communities, especially from one generation to the next.

In rural Britain traces of relatively peasantlike modes of life can still be found, but over the past fifty years, at least, the rural society in general has exhibited characteristics and trends which are progressively different from a peasant culture. The norms of behaviour and permissible actions have been broadened, and the thresholds of what is regarded as social deviancy have thus become widely spaced. In a total society which is undergoing relatively rapid and (on the basis of many indicators) accelerating change, this permeates to all sub-systems within our society. The detailed characteristics of the change processes, their modes of operation and their effectiveness may, in some respects, be different in the countryside compared to large towns and cities, but significant alterations are occurring throughout rural society.

The effects of an urbanised society on the rural population will be discussed in more detail later. However, much of the change which occurs may be regarded as largely proceeding *within* rural areas, implying various degrees of innovativeness among rural people, although the stimuli which initiate change may often originate in the urban sector. The kinds of changes which take place may be illustrated by considering some of the main processes of change at the level of the rural family, in particular of the farm family and farming, and of the village.

AGRICULTURAL CHANGE

Over most of the past three centuries or so, changes in agricultural technology have been occurring with increasing rapidity. Prior to the latter half of the last century much of this technological development depended on the inventive and imitative abilities of a relatively few farmers and rural craftsmen (although they were considerably more numerous than the quartet commonly mentioned in elementary history texts—Tull, Bakewell, Coke and Townshend). The improved ideas and practices thus originated slowly spread among farmers as a result of their observations of each others' activities, by word of mouth, and especially in the late eighteenth and early nineteenth centuries, through the conscious efforts to communicate knowledge about them by writers such as Arthur Young.

From the mid-nineteenth century onwards, more systematic research and development led to major improvements and inventions in farm mechanisation, crop varieties, artificial fertilisers and compound feeding stuffs. Increasingly, such technological advances have originated from work at universities and agricultural colleges, at research institutes, and by commercial manufacturers, or have been copied from the work of similar institutions in other countries, especially in north-west Europe (which had been the seat of many innovative agricultural ideas introduced into Britain as early as the sixteenth century) and North America. But inventors and improvers have continued to exist in local areas; for example, improvements to the efficiency of ploughs (in terms of local soils and topography), the development of improved strains of livestock, and the evolving of new farming systems have depended to a considerable extent on the activities of a minority of farmers. But the greater part of new technological developments in agriculture now arise from work at research institutes and similar centres, and by commercial firms, with active advocacy of their use by farmers through advertising in the agricultural Press, displays at agricultural shows and local demonstrations, the activities of salesmen, merchants and dealers, and not least, the efforts of professional agricultural advisers.

From the point of view of the individual farmer and his family, in most cases he has found himself in recent years inextricably involved in a situation comparable to a treadmill. In general terms, during the postwar period, as a result of a complex set of economic factors which affect most agricultural produce (including our national involvement in international trade in farm products, and the operation of government policies relating to British agriculture), the unit prices which farmers receive for their output have generally risen less rapidly than the production costs involved. To counteract the occurrence and prospect of a falling income, three broad reactions have been available to the farmer: first, to increase the scale of the farm business, which invariably has required considerable capital investment; secondly, to intensify production, generally by aiming for an improved technical performance from land and stock, mainly by the use of new or improved techniques and practices; and thirdly, to reduce production costs, the most obvious, quickest procedure having been to substitute capital (in the form of new machinery, equipment and other labour-saving devices and practices) for labour. Usually, various combinations of all three ways have been found on most farms, resulting in the growing productivity which has been apparent in the agricultural industry. But at the 'end' of the cycle, the real income of the farmer, in return for the acquisition and use of many advanced technological practices, the investment of considerable fixed and working capital, and the acquisition and exertion of much skill in manual tasks and farm management, may be little better. Thus the round continues.

Most farming decisions which face the farm family thus arise from a general problem, expressed as a felt need to maintain or improve its income and level of living (both in the immediate future and in the longer term), a problem which arises from the changing economic, political and technological environments of the total farming industry. At any one time, however, a farmer is likely to perceive a precisely located, specific need (for example, to increase the yield of a crop by eliminating some weed or pest, or to reduce the time required to undertake some task, or to be able to house and milk an enlarged dairy herd). In all cases, he requires a solution to *his* problem.

Members of the family, particularly any adult sons who are working at home or in partnership in the business, are likely to be influential in suggesting and discussing possible solutions. On larger holdings, employed workers may also be influential; as indicated earlier, the work force on even the largest farms is relatively small, and the relations between the farmer and employees is normally on a much more personal footing than is possible in most other work situations.

The decision-making process regarding any change involves an awareness and knowledge of the appropriate, available opportunities or solutions to a problem, selecting from among those which appear to be economically feasible in terms of the farmer's situation and farm characteristics, and the farm family's skills and interests. Before finally choosing, adequate information on several pertinent options will be required, so that a mental evaluation can be made and various decisions taken. But the process up to this point is rarely individualistic. A farmer's judgment is not solely a matter of his personal experience and the application of rational criteria. In addition to discussing the matter with the other members of the family and with his farm workers, he will inevitably be influenced by the actions of other farmers among his friends and neighbours, who have been or are faced with a similar problem, by various merchants and salesmen, and by the advice available from professional agricultural advisers and consultants. The latter include not only members of the Agricultural Development and Advisory Service of the Ministry of Agriculture, Fisheries and Food, and of the three agricultural colleges in Scotland, but also various private advisers, accountants, bank managers, solicitors, and the specialist technical advisers of commercial firms.

The intimate connections between family farming and the total life of the farm family makes it unlikely that decisions involving the farm are made independently of their anticipated implications for the whole family. The farm business, which is the source of the family's livelihood, might normally be expected to receive the highest priority. This is often the case, although the involvement of members of the family other than the farmer in a decision frequently changes the situation or delays it. For example, the need to replace a tractor may be considered not only in terms of available suitable makes and models of tractors, but also in relation to the wishes in the family to purchase a new car, or to remodel the farmhouse kitchen. Such a situation, which is very real in the farm family, is less likely to arise on the larger, commercial farms (often registered as companies), where the farm is viewed as a separate business, and where the farmer may vote himself and his family members a certain annual income.

After the family farmer has taken a decision to adopt some particular farming innovation (i.e. an idea or practice which is wholly or in part new to him), the change must be integrated into his farming system. In part this is a technical and economic matter of grafting a new element, often in substitution for an item being replaced, into his farming system. This often creates further problems, the solution of which requires the adoption of further technological innovations. There is evidence which suggests that anxieties arising from imaginatively anticipating the outcomes of adopting a specific innovation, outcomes which the farmer believes might require further changes (although they necessarily remain uncertain), are often sufficient to delay any serious consideration and decision concerning a solution to a recognised problem. The integration of an innovation by a farmer, however, is also a sociological process, in which the success and satisfaction derived from using it depend on the support and approbation of members of the family, of farm workers, and of farming friends and neighbours in the rural community.

The farm family, as such, also affects its own propensity to introduce farming and household changes in another way. The evidence from research studies in several developed countries concerning the relationship between farmers' ages and their willingness to change is somewhat inconsistent. One might expect that relatively young farmers, who tend to be better educated than their older counterparts and to whom the values implicit in modern technology are more acceptable, would be more ready to accept changes. To the extent that they do not always act as expected, which is frequently the case, the explanation rests largely in the developmental characteristics of the farm family.

Various ways have been suggested for dividing the life cycle of a family into several stages.[1] Six stages may be envisaged which bear a relationship to the acceptance of farming changes:

1. the relatively young married couple, starting on their own farm, at or soon after marriage;
2. young children, all under eleven years old;
3. some or all children are teenagers, all live at home but are in full-time education, but can assist with farm work on a casual basis;
4. some or all children, having completed their full-time education, are fully engaged in work on the farm;
5. children are marrying and being set up on farms or in careers of their own, unless remaining in partnership on home farm;
6. original couples on their own, unless one or more sons remain in partnership and progressively take over the farm's management.

During the first two stages, the main purpose of the young farmer and his wife must be to establish a viable farming unit to provide for their needs and those of their young family. On entering a farm, he may incorporate many up-to-date practices although (assuming he is a farmer's son, which most young farmers are) much of his view and knowledge of farming, his skills and interests are likely to have been developed on his father's farm. Learning from father still accounts for most of the training of young farmers, although increasing numbers are obtaining some form of full- or part-time vocational agricultural education. Further, strictly limited financial resources at these stages mean that the young farmer normally cannot adopt all applicable modern practices (even if he wishes to do so), while the needs of his family must necessarily receive a high priority.

As the children become teenagers, some assistance in farm work and a degree of interest in the farm business may be expected from them. By these middle stages in the family cycle, the viability of the business is likely to be well established, while the farmer, by now in middle age, can better afford to consider innovational changes which may further enhance his business.

As the stage of setting up his children on farms of their own, or in other careers, is reached, a drain is incurred on the farmer's resources with a consequent decline likely in changes which are possible on the home farm. Unless one or more sons remain at home in partnership with their father, it may be anticipated that as the farmer and his wife grow older their interest in further farming changes will tend to wane (except in so far as they appear inevitable due to social or economic pressures). Increasingly, farmers who are in partnership with sons may partially retire in their late sixties, but it is still common for family farmers to continue actively farming, occasionally with an enthusiasm for up-to-date methods and a keen business acumen, into their seventies and beyond.

So far, the effect of other farmers on any particular farmer's information, judgment, decision and action concerning agricultural innovations has only been partially indicated. Of major importance is the fact that all successful new ideas and practices diffuse gradually through the social system of farmers to whom they are applicable, whether this is considered nationally, regionally or locally. In the past, many innovations took a lengthy period to become universally accepted and used. For example, the use of the cereal reaper and binder spread gradually from the mid-nineteenth century to the 1920s, and the modern tractor from the 1930s to the late 1950s. In general, most new technological items, and to a lesser extent social innovations relevant in farming, diffuse much more rapidly today; several innovations and major improvements appear to be attaining almost universal acceptance among those farmers to whom they are applicable in under five years.

In any locality, a few farmers are invariably earlier than others to accept new ideas. Further, farmers generally in some rural communities or local areas are relatively more advanced and more innovative than others. To be among the first to accept an innovation, however rapid its complete diffusion may occur, is to be deviant to a degree, and thus to risk the sanctions invariably associated with deviancy. However, it should also be recognised that the actions of the pioneering, relatively early minority to accept particular innovations, 'the innovators', invariably have a pronounced influence (directly or indirectly, positively or negatively) on the reactions of later adopters. This is true both in terms of farmers within one rural community, and in broader terms between rural communities. The concepts and findings which have emerged from research into decision-making regarding innovations, and their diffusion, particularly as a consequence of large numbers of rural sociological studies mainly into the processes as they operate in the adoption by farmers of agricultural innovations, can only be briefly touched upon in this chapter; for more detailed discussions, reference should be made to Jones[2] and Rogers and Shoemaker.[3]

In simplified form, the diffusion of an innovation among farmers may be visualised as its cumulative and increasingly widespread adoption (Fig. 16). Some communities, reflecting values and norms which are relatively favourable towards innovation and change, may exhibit a rapid and relatively early diffusion (curve B), where in terms of the national spread of an innovative item (curve

A) most if not all farmers would be classed as innovators. But amongst themselves, on the basis of their relative time of adoption within their community, some farmers are innovators, some are laggards. Similarly, in more 'backward' communities (curve C),

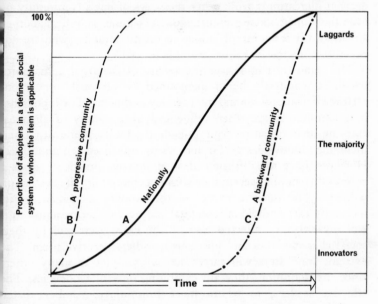

Fig. 16   Simplified diffusion curves and adopter categories for an innovation. A nationally; B a 'progressive' community; C a 'backward' community

where few if any have started using a particular practice until it is in widespread use nationally, again internally a minority would be regarded as innovators. A diffusion model of this kind is applicable in most situations where a large number of potential adopters of an item exist; it is equally appropriate in considering the adoption of household equipment and practices among farmers' wives, and indeed for all consumer behaviour.

Compared to the later adopters, the innovators are invariably individuals who are able to make competent use of, and rely mainly on, more specialised, more technical, and often more specific sources of information concerning innovations. As the innovation spreads through the majority and towards the laggards, information about it which is regarded as usable and credible is generally derived increasingly from other members of one's community or even the immediate neighbourhood. In farming, as well as in other activities, the influence of leaders in the community (who are not necessarily themselves innovators) is crucial.

This again re-emphasises the reality of the rural community which is manifestly being maintained by personal interaction, reciprocal relationships and interpersonal influence. The innovators in a community are often influenced by a variety of channels carrying in information from outside the local community, often including innovators in other more advanced communities. However, once the diffusion of an innovative practice reaches a certain threshold of acceptance within a community, its evaluation will rarely be solely a matter of the rational assessment of its merits by each individual potential adopter; rather, reaction to it will invariably be affected also by the early users and by their social characteristics and positions as others perceive them. The extreme innovators will rarely act as examples to many others since, by definition, they are exhibiting deviant tendencies. The effective leaders, to whom most community members listen regarding their experiences with and reactions to an innovation, who are believed, and who can justify the rightness of its acceptance and use by others (and who can thus affect a change in local values concerning the new) are more likely to be found among the later innovators or those who are early within the majority. Of course these community leaders will have been influenced to some degree by adopters who were earlier; the actions of innovators are crucial largely because they not only introduce new ideas into a community but also succeed in influencing the effective leaders. Moreover these leaders, who influence others in a completely informal manner and who may be performing this function unintentionally (and even unconsciously), often also believe that for them to be extreme innovators could adversely affect their social position

Over time, the incumbents of such informal leadership positions do change, sometimes because they have become too innovative in the opinion of their neighbours and other members of the community, sometimes as a result of their involvement in other kinds of actions which lead to a loss of status and prestige within the community. In addition, others acquire leadership roles as a result of their actions and abilities within or outside the community.

NEIGHBOURHOOD AND COMMUNITY CHANGE

The preceding discussion of the nature of agricultural change, which depends so much on social interaction within a rural community and between communities, illustrates many of the essentials in the dynamics of rural life. This is particularly apparent in the process of technological change in farming, involving interaction among farmers, eventually from the largest commercial businesses to the small part-time farmers. As indicated earlier, similar processes operate in the adoption of new items by farmers' wives and among consumers in general. They also occur in numerous other aspects of life. The processes of change in social activities, as well as in services and amenities, operate in somewhat comparable ways. Social innovations which often originate in urban areas diffuse not only to other towns and cities but also to the countryside from the urban centres; but the process does not always occur in this direction. For example, Pedley has shown that for secondary schools of a broadly comprehensive character 'first in time, and in recruitment more comprehensive that anything London and the other big cities can show, come the rural areas', if only for reasons of 'hard economics and practical efficiency';[4] of nearly 240 secondary schools of this kind in 1962, one-sixth of those in rural Wales existed by 1949 and by 1952 in the English counties, compared to 1955 before the same proportion was achieved in the cities.

Social action at a community level and decision-making concerning the acceptance of some change or new activity by a parish council, village committee, or meeting of a group of neighbours, involves somewhat more complex processes than for an individual or family. The basic reason for giving consideration to a change is likely to arise from a felt need among at least some sector of the community (often the young people, or any new-comers, or the accepted local leaders). To this extent they act as internal 'change agents', providing more or less valid information which is essential in the community's decision-making. Relative newcomers to a community are especially important in this context, and are often somewhat comparable to innovators regarding new ideas and practices open to individual adoption. As newcomers they are likely to carry with them knowledge of community activities in another area. Moreover, the new community they have entered invariably recognises their role as potential deviants, while if any proposal they originate is accepted, but is later found to be a failure, they can be blamed without destroying the established cohesiveness of the community. Specific, valid, relevant information concerning social innovations, however, is commonly much less available than, for example, that required by a farmer considering some agricultural innovation or improvement. The officers of county councils and other bodies may often be able to provide information and advice on the feasibility of locally desired changes, and support may be available in the form of financial assistance as well as guidance. But so far, the provision of such an advisory function, nor a recognition of the need for it, is not highly developed.

Any proposals involving a formal group discussion among villagers and rural dwellers, as everywhere, is likely to face a range of arguments for and against. But more than in urban contexts, influence and leadership within a meeting which are heavily dependent on relationships and recognised positions of status role outside the formal gathering, will normally be crucial in deter-mining the form of the decision-making process and the decision reached in a rural community. Landowners and farmers, as well as certain important individuals, such as the clergyman, Non-conformist minister, school-teacher, and any other local profes-sional people, have traditionally provided the greater part of rural leadership, although today this appears to be dispersed progressively more widely within most rural communities. However, in any social discussion and action, the local norms governing behaviour, and a recognition of the likely effects of any action on existing local institutions and organisations, as well as on individuals, will invariably act as a control on any decisions taken. This can act either to foster or to retard any changes.

If a proposal under discussion is already in operation in another local village, neighbourhood or community, this fact will inevitably enter into the discussion. Few villages are so closed to outside influences that life within them is conducted in complete ignorance of changes and developments in surrounding areas. But the effect may not always be to stimulate the wider acceptance of change; social tensions between localities may inhibit any imitation. Conversely, friendly rivalry among villages may encourage copying. Varying degrees and kinds of innovativeness and of leadership exist among neighbourhoods and villages. Informal visits will often be made by residents of one community to another which is an earlier adoption of a particular social innovation has occurred in order to gain information and to discuss the practical issues involved. A more or less local diffusion process again complements and supports decision-making at the level of the community or neighbourhood as the potential adoption unit. Finally, if a new community item or activity is adopted, probably after a general meeting of interested inhabitants, its presence has to be integrated into the community life, involving a continuing interest and public service by various individuals.

This kind of process, leading to significant social changes in rural communities, can be observed in a wide range of examples. During the latter half of the nineteenth century, various village clubs and reading rooms spread among British villages. Similarly, church reconstructions or improvements, the erection of village halls, the provision of various sports facilities, and the introduction of a variety of public services and amenities, have diffused widely among rural communities during this century. These and many other examples are of the nature of an innovation to each particular village or community when they are first adopted. Their introduction has often resulted in realignments in existing social relationships. They may also recreate old tensions or lead to new ones within a community, which, unless it leads to excessive energy being expended in local social conflict, may be beneficial in encouraging further change and adaptation within a community towards a mode of life which its people desire. But many rural community changes also have been, and continue to be, the result of local initiative, planning and action directed towards satisfying a recognised need. The overall effect of change, involving processes of the kinds described, is usually to reinforce social cohesion within the community and the acceptance of its validity as a basis for the life of its inhabitants.

Rural-urban interaction and rural change

Contemporary Britain is an urban and an urbanised nation. The majority of the population lives in an urban or suburban environment; many residents in the countryside travel daily to work or for other purposes to relatively large towns and cities. Moreover, urban influences penetrate easily and consistently into rural areas. In England, in particular, the greater part of the area is near and easily accessible to urban concentrations, virtually in the shadow of the larger towns and cities (Fig. 17). Regions in England and Wales regarded as 'rural' by Green[1] are on the whole more remote from such urban centres, or are areas where access to the few larger towns or cities is often difficult due to the topography or lack of public transport or both. Only in the south Midlands, largely west Northamptonshire, north Oxfordshire, north Gloucestershire, west Berkshire and Wiltshire, is there an area which is distinctly rural yet comparatively near to sizeable urban centres (Green's "South Central England rural region").

It is perhaps not surprising, therefore, that social scientists whose focus of interest is urban, as well as many civil servants, local government officers and politicians, view rural areas as mere appendages to the towns and cities, and consider their inhabitants and their problems as amenable for discussion and solution in terms similar to those employed in the urban context. It is true that a great deal of rural life proceeds under innumerable, constant and direct urban influences, and this is likely to occur to an increasing extent, over an expanding area, in the future. But for various sound reasons, one of the more immediate being the currently proposed realignment of local government areas, based broadly on the major urban centres (albeit not the 'city regions' which many commentators would have wished), the need to

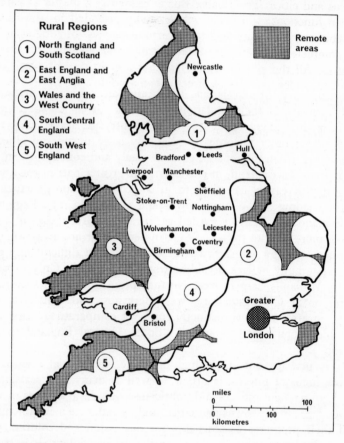

Rural Regions

1 North England and South Scotland
2 East England and East Anglia
3 Wales and the West Country
4 South Central England
5 South West England

Remote areas

Fig. 17 Large towns and remote areas, and 'rural regions' in England and Wales
'Remote areas' denote areas more than 30 miles from a town of over 250,000 inhabitants, or 20 miles from a town of over 50,000 to 250,000 inhabitants in 1966.

recognise and understand the changing rural situation is crucial.

As already discussed, the inhabitants of rural communities rely to a large extent on the services available to them in nearby towns and cities. To visualise this as primarily a matter of using urban functions, which are only partially provided for the rural inhabitants, can easily lead to the erroneous view of rural society as completely dependent, economically and socially, on such centres. All the evidence indicates that a great deal of rural life proceeds independently of direct urban stimulus. Moreover, such dependence as does exist is by no means only in one direction. The towns and cities draw a significant part of their labour and trade, and participation in their social and recreational activities, from surrounding rural areas, while a substantial sector of the services they contain has arisen in response to rural needs. This is true not only regarding agricultural services (such as livestock markets and agricultural merchants) or those parts of general and professional services (such as banking, accountancy, etc.) which are provided for farmers. The non-agricultural rural people are also important customers and clients, often at a higher level per head or per family than is usual among urban dwellers in the area. An interdependence of town and countryside exists. This is nothing new in Britain, since it has been a traditional phenomenon since the Middle Ages. Today, however, it differs even in comparison with the early part of this century in its extent and character, and it is continuously changing.

Many rural changes arise from needs which are more or less internal to a rural social system, as indicated in the last chapter. Yet many of the basic reasons for such changes and the main apparent forces affecting them are of urban origin. But it is important to recognise this as emerging from a reaction by rural dwellers to the urban situation as they perceive it or growing out of an urban reaction to earlier changes among the rural population. It is a continuing process of action and reaction. Increasingly, more and more rural change can be regarded as arising from influences which, in an immediate sense, originate externally to the rural community as such.

UNPLANNED CHANGE

Much of this change is of an unplanned kind. It is the result of normal social contact and interaction between rural and urban people, in which the direct effects of the towns and cities frequented by rural inhabitants are important. A diffusion to rural communities of various kinds of behaviours, activities and styles of life, initially associated with towns and cities, has for a long time been common in Britain, although rural selectivity and the adaptation of any imitations often lead to versions among the country people which are markedly different from their urban equivalents.

British rural people are thus open to receive and accept a multitude of urban influences, to as great an extent as in any developed country. The mass media are important factors in this process, having a universal effect throughout our society. Radio and television exist as commonly in the countryside as in towns and cities. National daily newspapers may not be received as frequently in some remoter rural areas, but regional daily and more local weekly newspapers are widely read. There is no evidence to suggest that rural inhabitants today are in general any less informed than urban dwellers about news of national and international happenings, or take any less interest in the recreation and entertainment available through the mass media. However, in a social situation where personal interaction still matters to a high degree, a somewhat more localite or parochial interpretation of the content of the media is inevitable. This also occurs in parts of urban society, but for the rural community events in distant urban centres, or entertainments provided in a 'city style', appear to have less relevance.

Yet in the past twenty years or so, one of the most significant changes in rural life has been the broader, less local, more urbanised outlook which has evolved, largely as a result of the mass media (and a deeper appreciation of much of their content as a consequence generally of higher levels of education received). This is particularly apparent among the younger generation of rural inhabitants. This means that, as much as at any time in the past, their real life continues to be different from their imaginative world of urban life and urbanised ways of living. Moreover, it has a pronounced positive effect on the willingness among rural people to accept change, even to desire change. It helps to produce varying degrees of dissatisfaction with their present situation, which is a basic condition for producing social change in all societies.

For the individual or single family, two main ways are open to solve any problems which are recognised in the local rural situation or any discontent felt concerning it. First, possible improvements in it may be perceived, leading to attempts to initiate action towards achieving them; but such action is usually only possible by becoming involved in group action, or participating in the united efforts of some sectors of the community. It invariably means political action and establishing a dialogue with various authorities. Secondly, it is possible to move away to a different situation which is imagined and expected to be 'better'; but this requires making what is invariably a difficult decision. It frequently means movement to an urban area.

The latter continues to be the solution chosen by many individuals and families in rural areas which, especially in remoter, upland areas, has often resulted in rural depopulation. This occurs not only from individuals feeling they are being 'pushed out' of their present home and community due to a lack of suitable employment or inadequate possibilities to achieve a desired level of income or of services; there is also the felt attraction of other areas based on information which is rarely complete or even adequate, possessed about those areas. Both processes are usually present, and can be regarded as traditional and normal over much of rural Britain. Population movement has been proceeding at a rate which has resulted in a declining total population in many rural areas since the middle of the last century, with many consequent changes in their demographic and social structures.[2] In the past, knowledge of urban life and opportunities reached the countryside mainly by means of letters from earlier migrants and periodic return visits to their home area. The destination of movement from one extended family or local community was thus often to those urban and industrial areas to which relatives and friends had moved earlier. This is still important, but nowadays, the rural dweller's partial knowledge and image of urban life is also being provided to a large extent by the mass media and by short temporary visits made to larger towns and cities. Similarly, it should be noted, much of the movement of urban dwellers to live in the countryside, which is such a pronounced feature in those rural areas accessible to the major urban centres, also results in some measure from an unrealistic image of rural living presented by the mass media.

The situation for a relatively remote region, with a low population density, which is predominantly rural, has been clearly shown in a Government report on 'the most extensive area in England and Wales showing rural depopulation', namely Mid-Wales.[3] Over most of the area, the population has been continuously declining throughout this century and longer, at a rate which, in several parts of the area, has accelerated in the past twenty years; the decline is especially marked if compared to the growing total population of Wales and in the administrative rural districts as a whole in England and Wales (Table 9). In an aggravated form, the problems of the area are similar to those of most rural areas which experience depopulation.

The increasing efficiency of agriculture, especially since the late 1940s, and an agricultural policy which on the whole has been less favourable to hill farming, have meant that fewer agricultural workers have been required. In the absence of alternative local employment, movement out of the area is inevitable. Moreover, the low and decreasing density of the population, its changing structure and its dispersed distribution, makes such a region relatively unattractive to industrial development, despite Government inducements to locate new industry there. The continuing high dependence upon agriculture for local employment in Mid-Wales is reflected in income levels which are relatively low by national standards and relatively high levels of unemployment. In turn, these accelerate further outward migration, with further dispersal of families, an impoverishment of rural social life, and individual and community frustration arising from feelings of

TABLE 9
Total population changes in Mid-Wales, 1901–71

	1901	1951	1961	1971*	Percentage population change per decade		
					1901–51	1951–61	1961–71
Mid-Wales area	215,492	185,729	178,546	174,089	− 2.8	− 3.9	− 2.5
Breconshire (part)	27,380	25,003	23,952	22,945	− 1.7	− 4.2	− 4.2
Cardiganshire	61,078	53,278	53,648	54,844	− 2.6	+ 0.7	+ 2.2
Merionethshire	48,852	41,465	38,310	35,277	− 3.0	− 7.6	− 7.9
Montgomeryshire	54,901	45,990	44,165	42,761	− 3.2	− 4.0	− 3.2
Radnorshire	23,281	19,993	18,471	18,262	− 2.9	− 7.6	− 1.1
Wales	1,943,648	2,598,675	2,644,023	2,723,596	+ 6.7	+ 1.7	+ 3.0
England and Wales	32,527,843	43,757,888	46,104,548	48,593,658	+ 6.9	+ 5.4	+ 5.4
Administrative rural districts in England and Wales+	not available	8,193,446	8,953,927	10,568,303		+10.9	+11.8
Administrative rural districts in Mid-Wales+	not available	116,620	109,745	104,437		− 5.9	− 4.8

*provisional figures
+as defined in 1971

relative deprivation. However, the provision of public services, even at comparatively low standards, becomes relatively costly and requires a higher subsidy than elsewhere from central government funds. At individual and community levels, even with a variety of efforts (which are on the whole uncoordinated) to ameliorate the situation, the process tends to be cumulative. As the report states:

> Available information suggests that a primary cause of outward migration is the lack of employment opportunities and, certainly, of any specialised employment opportunities within the existing community. This lack may be due to the decline or changing pattern of the basic industries. Nowadays other reasons, perhaps equally as valid or even stronger, are, for example, dissatisfaction with existing living conditions, the attractions of the big city and the urge of the younger age groups for an increased tempo of life. Perhaps the most important aspect of outward migration is that it removes a large proportion of that element of the population possessing the greatest talents and initiative in the way of social leadership and economic drive. . . . The result of this process of denudation has been to leave a residue, a high proportion of whom, particularly amongst the small owner-occupier farms, can be regarded as marginal . . . in the sense that they would meet further economic adversity by reducing yet lower their standard of living. Thus one of the main consequences of outward migration has been to produce this hard core of the farming community, lacking in financial resources and supported by a minority of secondary population and isolated miscellaneous groups, many of whom suffer from the same deficiencies. (*Depopulation in Mid-Wales*,[3] p. 70, paras. 254 and 255).

PLANNED CHANGE

While some degree of change is a normal phenomenon in all rural areas, where the pace is relatively rapid and its extent marked, conscious adaptations to new situations are necessary. Such is the case both in rural areas experiencing a rapidly increasing population, usually resulting from earlier planning decisions, and in areas witnessing depopulation, which is often less directly related to planning. In both situations, the need is for further and continuing positive planning in order to achieve adaptations which are appropriate to the changing size and structure of the population. In particular, adaptations become necessary in each rural community's social and economic provisions and organisations.

In addition to necessary changes to satisfy the alterations in the needs of rural inhabitants, including not only farmers, horticulturalists, their workers and forestry workers (who seek a livelihood from enterprises which are economically and technically modern and viable and who wish to live within range of up-to-date services and amenities) but also all other villagers, many other voices have in recent years been exerting various pressures on the character of rural areas. Many of the basic issues are currently combined under the comprehensive heading of the relationships between the national society and the countryside, although it is essential to distinguish the various elements involved.[4] These range from a variety of conservationists, who are often basically preservationists out of self-interest or some specific field of interest (whether it be concerned with the biological habitat or, less commonly, the traditional elements of rural life) to those which to have access to and use of the countryside for a variety of recreational purposes. In passing, it should be noted that many farmers, landowners and other natives of rural communities claim, with considerable justification, that they have always aimed to conserve the rural landscape (which is not the same as to preserve an anachronism) as matters of good agricultural husbandry and local pride in their neighbourhoods. This has occurred despite intense economic pressures to produce food as cheaply as possible and a cost of living which, in several aspects, is relatively high in rural areas. To reconcile the many various demands is extremely difficult. Attempts to do so have led to much confusion and often to conflicts between apparently opposed interests (such as the four-sided arguments between farmers, foresters, biological conservationists, and recreation-seekers in several upland areas). However, the rural society is not resistant to change as such; its adaptations in innumerable unplanned ways to a changing society is evidence of this. But, more than at any time in the past, guidance and leadership, based on the use of valid knowledge and the active involvement of all who are directly affected, is necessary.

Varying degrees of planning are now dominant in shaping the character of rural life. This implies that a predetermination has occurred of which facilities shall exist and of socially relevant actions towards achieving them, based on conscious decision-making. It is apparent to some extent in the attempts to satisfy urban demands on the countryside and its inhabitants. It is present in the changing distribution of the rural population. It also operates, though somewhat less directly regarding specific rural areas, in the application of a variety of government policies, especially agricultural policy, as they take effect at regional and more local levels.

A tradition of 'town and country planning' exists in Britain which stretches back at least to the early years of this century. However, its emphasis has been on the whole urban based and urban oriented. Even planning concerning the countryside has often contained within it an implicit urban point of view towards rural issues. It has generally appeared to rural people, and become a firmly held belief among them, that decisions affecting new buildings in villages, or the siting of proposed facilities and services (such as new or improved roads, or schools), or the withdrawal of certain services (especially of public transport), have been decided solely on urban (which are often spoken of as 'national') criteria and standards. Consequently planning is often viewed as an opposing force and negative. It is difficult to avoid the conclusion that, at the level of rural neighbourhoods and villages, most inhabitants are of the opinion either that their village is 'open', that it should be allowed to grow (at least up to a point), and that it should be fully provided with necessary services, or, much more rarely nowadays, that they should be left alone, to make only those changes which they themselves wish but free from all 'outside interference'.

It is only very recently that a degree of mutual determination of planned change has begun to occur, involving the relevant rural population as well as elected government representatives and the planners (as local or national government officers). The Town and Country Planning Act of 1968 provides for the direct involvement of the public in the planning process. Especially since the publication of the Skeffington Committee Report (1969),[5] guidelines have become available for the means by which the public might be encouraged to participate *effectively*, in order to achieve planning processes which are efficient (not frustrating either to the public or to the planners), acceptable and satisfying (in the sense that they do not lead to acrimony or hostility), while the decisions are recognised as equitable.

It is impossible to consider here the multitude of situations where planning already affects rural communities. Rather, it is more relevant to present a view of the main aims of rural planning and the means by which change may be attained in satisfactory ways. Its main aims are essentially to attempt to reconcile competing uses of the land, conserving the character and beauty of the countryside, and redistributing the rural population so as to produce settlements which are both economically and socially viable, and communities with an adequate institutional and organisational base.[6] If planning policies 'are based on a thorough analysis of currently available information and are comprehensive, positive and constructive rather than piecemeal, negative and purely defensive they will achieve not only conservation where it is merited, but also the creation of character in settlements where at present there is little or none'.[7] The planning staffs of various local authorities have admirably demonstrated their ability to do this in their county development plans and in numerous local and village plans.

However, in any democratic planning process, the people to be affected must know and understand what is intended, while from the side of the planners, the aims and aspirations of the people who are being planned for need to be distinguished and taken into account. In the rural context, the eventual desired results must be different in most respects from those pertaining in urban areas if the community is to remain rural in character. The rural ideal today, which would be supported by many recent newcomers into rural communities from urban areas, is to be able to live where the everyday needs of work and social intercourse are available and accessible, without being submerged by suburban-type expansion nor an excessive seasonal influx of tourists. Over much of England, at least, the physical suburbanisation of the countryside would be all too likely without planning and an acceptable level of control. Perceptive planning, providing information and guidance, is necessary in order to stimulate adaptations to changing situations among country people, which are acceptable to them. This is envisaged in the proposals applicable to local government authorities embodied in the Skeffington Report, and is being successfully attempted in various contexts by the Countryside Commission and other agencies operating in rural areas. A lack of planning based on consultation, mutual understanding and realistic anticipation can only lead to further problems and conflicts between rural and urban interests in the future.

The mutual determination of objectives and means for their attainment, which is fundamental to a process of planned change that is not intended to be, nor to be seen as being technocratic or coercive, is new to local planning in Britain. Throughout this century, planners have continuously been major agents of change, possibly more in terms of areas and their landscapes than of sectors of society, although their effect on rural society has been profound. The approach being advocated here is more socially directed. If it is to succeed, planners must see their role as including aspects of community development. In the past in Britain (though not in many other European countries and North America) the term 'community development' has conjured up visions of villagers being consciously 'helped to help themselves' in some developing country or, more recently, social work in the slum areas of our larger urban centres and in new towns. The approach, suitably modified, is equally valid in normal rural situations in Britain.

This is an approach implicit in the proposals for stimulating public participation in planning contained in the Skeffington

Commitee Report, but it involves more than merely consulting citizens for their views on plans prepared for their home area. More fundamentally it includes helping people who live within areas which are socially meaningful to recognise the problems of their locality and community within the context of wider areas and sectors of society. This is essentially an educational process based on information, guidance and discussion, which seeks to discover ways in which people can and will become involved in social action for their own benefit, as individuals and as communities. A continuing dialogue between planners and the public in country areas, which itself leads to a greater understanding by each of the other, is an essential element in effective rural development.

AGRICULTURAL POLICY AND CHANGE

Planning, but of a different kind, also affects agriculture specifically through the construction and operation of government agricultural policy. Change and development in agriculture depend not only on individual farmers' resources, interests, knowledge and abilities (discussed in the previous chapter), but also on the economic support and intellectual investment (which has been defined as a compound of research, education, information, promotion and influences) which farmers as a whole receive largely from the government. Attention has already been drawn to some of the effects of agricultural policies on farmers, but these arise and operate in rather different ways to the plans devised by local government planners.

In most developed countries, the case for a strong agricultural policy, which invariably contains not only several economic facets but also government provision or support of agricultural research and advisory work, arises to a large extent from the structure of agriculture. The aim, at least in part, explicitly or implicitly, is to assure certain levels of income, wellbeing and continued development for farmers and their families.

Compared to most other production industries, farmers as

producers are relatively numerous and small in scale, and therefore as individuals possess only weak power in their relations with the comparatively few merchants and wholesalers whom they supply. Further, because of each farmer's relative small size within the whole industry, it is impossible for individuals (even the larger farmers) to undertake their own research and internal service of advice to management. In most cases the farmer himself is both a manual worker and the manager and owner of his farm. In addition, because of the inelastic nature of the demand at any one time facing most agricultural products (especially the basic food products), the more that is produced the lower tends to be the price received by the farmer. In theory at least, if uncontrolled this could lead to violent swings in the total British farm production of most products, to the detriment of consumers as well as the producers. Although the dominant aspects of an agricultural policy thus usually appear to be economic, it also contains other components. As a whole it strongly affects the social structure of farming and of rural communities.

This is in no sense a recent development. Government policies have in various ways affected agriculture in Britain over at least the past three centuries. However, the traditional rural bias in parliamentary representation, on which farmers relied, no longer exists; the significance of the 'agricultural vote' at general elections (even assuming all farmers were to unite politically) is now minimal except in a few marginal rural seats. During this century, agricultural legislation and policy have become both more complex and specific, in which farmers' interests have been represented increasingly by the main farmers' unions. The result has been various Acts of Parliament which have aimed to reconcile farmers' demands with those of the nation (e.g. the smallholdings acts of the late nineteenth century, the agricultural marketing acts of the early 1930s which allowed the creation of producers' marketing boards, and legislation covering security of tenure and 'fair' prices since the war) as well as a variety of schemes to assist the economy and development of farms through grants, price supports and import restrictions.[8] Since the 1939–45 war the various subsidies have mainly been determined by the Government, in consultation with the farmers' unions, at annual reviews of the industry.

In a general sense, such legislation and government schemes have affected all farmers, although, over the years, their emphasis has been altered and their impact has varied. Changes at different times in the ratios of farmers' costs to supported prices have been determined intentionally so as to be more favourable to some farm enterprises and products than to others, or to certain areas, or to certain types or systems or scales of farming. The emphasis on maximum food production at almost any cost during and immediately after the 1939–45 war led to prices and other stimuli being sufficient for farmers to reclaim and improve upland grazing areas, and to maintain relatively small holdings which provided a living for a family. Since the middle 'fifties, the stated need has been to produce farm products at prices which would not lead to the agricultural support provided by the Treasury becoming excessive. Relatively lower prices, coupled with the rising trend in the costs to farmers of employed labour and purchased farm requisites, have led to a reduction in the number of full-time farms, especially small-sized holdings, and progressively higher levels of productivity on those remaining.

The changing nature of economic policies affecting agriculture in recent years, and in the foreseeable future, involving less direct support of agricultural prices and more control of food imports, means that consumer prices are likely to rise, although the tax burden of guaranteed prices for farmers will diminish. Also, since the Agriculture Act of 1967 the Government has tried to stimulate more, and more varied, forms of cooperation and joint action among farmers. The effects of new policies on the character of British farming are as difficult to predict as at any time during the past quarter of a century. The results of particular policies have often turned out to have various unanticipated consequences or responses from farmers as a whole, occasionally even in an opposite direction to the presupposed effect. One thing is certain— all farmers do not react solely, directly or immediately to government policy or exhortation, nor to price movements; the variety of personal, situational and sociological factors which affect the adoption and its timing of more technological changes amply demonstrate this.

The active sponsorship by governments since the 1930s of applied scientific research in agriculture (through work at the institutes of the Agricultural Research Council and research and development activities in universities), as well as research conducted by commercial manufacturers of agricultural requisites and in recent years by farmers' marketing boards and commodity authorities, leads to continuous additions and improvements to the knowledge and techniques available to farmers and their workers. The generally higher level of education obtained by younger farmers, and currently being received by farm children, also positively affects their adaptability and responsiveness to available changes. Compared to any period in the past, farmers are more business-minded and more adaptable to changing technological and economic situations. Various new organisational forms, involving farm management, marketing, and local area development have become common among farmers, in some areas even a norm. This reflects a trend towards more *Gesellschaft*-like ways of life and work, an urbanisation of farmers in several socio-psychological and sociological respects. This is more than a simple reaction to national policies and their economic and technological outcomes. It also involves more intensive relationships between farmers and various institutions associated with urban life.

The situation may be typified by the family farmer who, in addition to the urban influences which reach most rural dwellers, is also affected by many channels of communication which are specifically concerned with agriculture. In many ways these maintain an ambivalent position in that they aim to be part of the agricultural social system while also, necessarily, being part of an urban social system. The national and regional farming journals, one or more of which are received regularly by most farmers, are based editorially in London or one of the large provincial cities. Many farmers' clubs, meetings and agricultural shows, take place in urban surroundings. The agricultural advisory services at ational and regional levels are mainly based at or near the larger cities. The linkages which they create between modern knowledge and farmers are an important form of rural–urban interaction. On the whole they are highly successful—the diffusion of many agricultural innovations bears witness to this.

'Community' studies of British rural localities, even those in which considerable attention has been given to farm families and farming institutions, have neglected the impact of agricultural advisory work among farmers. Since the second half of the last century, when the scientific study of agriculture became more systematic, conscious efforts have been made to disseminate results which could be of value to farmers. Research effort, whether it is concerned with the solution of problems which are apparent within, or likely to occur within agriculture, or whether it is motivated and guided by the initiative of scientists and technologists, would be largely frustrated if the resulting innovations and improvements were not adopted by farmers. Thus agricultural scientists, and later agricultural teachers and advisers, have been increasingly available for over a century to answer farmers' problems and to assist farm development. During the interwar period, a close association existed between agricultural education at county farm institutes, agricultural colleges and university departments of agriculture, and the provision of agricultural information and advice; the teaching and advisory staff were often the same. Since the war, this system has basically continued in Scotland, but in England and Wales new advisory services, largely dissociated from agricultural educational institutions, have been established within the Ministry of Agriculture, Fisheries and Food. In Northern Ireland, links between advisory work and education have also been retained. In 1971 the various Ministry advisory and technical services provided in England and Wales were combined to form the Agricultural Development and Advisory Service.

The impact on farmers and rural life of the agricultural advisory work by these agencies and their staffs during the past quarter of a century, together with the effects of salesmen and technical

advisers from commercial firms, and in recent years the growir
numbers of other agricultural advisers (either within farmer
organisations, such as the Milk Marketing Boards, or priva
practitioners), can only be partially assessed. Much of the chang
and development which has occurred in farm husbandry practice
in farming systems and organisation, in farm managemer
practices and the business-orientation of farmers and their familie
is due in large measure to their work. They have advocated chang
and helped farmers to resolve problems by adapting to changin
situations, and to overcome difficulties involved in such adaptatior
and they have encouraged farmers to seek higher levels of pro
ductivity. It is true that farmers have been responding to gener:
economic pressures by reducing labour, adopting new technolog
reorganising their farming systems, and changing their scale
or intensities of production; economists can demonstrate th
validity of this response. It is also true that most individu:
farmers would have had insufficient knowledge or manageri:
ability to know what courses of feasible action were open to the
without the help and guidance of advisers.

The focus of advisory work has not only been at the lev
of the individual farmer. As change agents, the methods whic
advisers have employed to stimulate farming development ha
often been based upon processes of planned change, similar t
those advocated earlier in the context of local planning, involvin
a mutual determination by a farmer and his adviser of objective
or ideally required outcome; the adviser has usually been able t
suggest solutions to the farmer's problems in so far as usabl
knowledge and practices exist, or has transmitted the problem fo
investigation to specialist advisers or research workers. Th
advisory services have also done much to stimulate the formatio
of farmers' groups for discussion and joint action. To the exten
that they have helped to improve the income levels of farm families
to reduce the hired labour force on British farms, and to create
more business-minded farm population, they have also criticall
affected the social structure of rural communities.

Among farmers, however, it is still rare to discover the complet absence of certain norms and values which have been associated traditionally with agriculture. Despite all attachments with urban ways of life, and despite accepting much new scientific knowledge and modern technology, including the production processes required by them, family farmers on the whole remain recognisably rural. They tend to give a high value to independence (a value also dominant among farm workers who are rarely involved in routine or group-work activities) and to other characteristics associated with farming. For example, attempts in recent years to foster formal types of cooperation among farmers have in many respects been disappointing, especially among smaller farmers who could benefit economically to a marked extent. Farmers generally adhere to norms and values that are implicit in the good husbandry of land, crops and livestock. Extreme or even moderate abuses of agricultural production processes, especially in livestock production (so-called 'factory farming'), are rare, and more of an urban myth than a reality among farmers. The generally good health of livestock and high quality of agricultural products attest to this. Moreover, most farmers express genuine abhorrence at the image of modern farming which has often been created by expressions such as 'mass' or 'factory' production. An increasingly high degree of urbanisation has become a general characteristic especially among more innovative farmers, but this is not a wholesale acceptance of urban ways and values. Rather, it reflects interaction with, and often varied experiences of, urban life which allow the farmer to judge critically and select from among the urban influences which bear upon him.

Throughout this chapter, the aim has been to indicate that, in a variety of ways, influences which arise externally to the rural community are of prime importance in bringing about change within it. This is in no way to minimise the importance of internal forces discussed in the last chapter. Rather it indicates that rural change and development in Britain arise from a complex interaction between urban and rural life, and that the conflicts and tensions produced, as much as the support of the one for the other, are necessary conditions for further internal adaptations.

Future prospects

Once upon a time, not so very long ago, rural life in Britain appeared almost unchanging. Many older rural inhabitants can still genuinely recall the time when tradition and custom were dominant. This is not to say that no changes of social significance ever occurred. Rather, for the majority of rural dwellers their ways of life and living changed relatively little from one year to the next, considerably more from one generation to the next, but rarely more than could be easily integrated by the existing local culture. Villages grew and decayed, even disappeared, over a span of several centuries. Changes also occurred slowly in the patterns and emphases in farming in response to national economic circumstances, while occasional agricultural innovations were introduced and accepted. Some more rapid rural changes, mainly associated with industrial development, were very localised and abnormal.

As recently as 1945 the late Dr C. S. Orwin, after a lifetime of observing and studying British agricultural organisation, farm and rural life, could state that in general little real change had occurred in the rural scene since the late nineteenth century.[1] He imagined a British equivalent of Rip van Winkle, a farmer, who had fallen asleep some sixty years earlier in his home area, somewhere in rural England well away from the shadow of a large urban centre. On awakening in the early 1940s he would have found very few changes in the rural landscape (the field patterns, the country lanes, the farm houses and buildings, farming practices) or in the village (its buildings, layout, amenities) which would have been incomprehensible to him. Imagining the scene for another Rip van Winkle who, falling asleep in 1940 was to awake a generation later, Orwin foresaw considerable change, which in general terms and in many specific ways have been verified by the passage of time. The rural problems which he recognised towards the end of the Second World War indicated the need for many changes, while the means to their solution were abundantly clear and accepted, and the significant trends sufficiently strong to assure their occurrence. As he foresaw, many of the changes would result from the diffusion of urban facilities, influences and modes of life into the countryside.

In areas very near to the larger cities this process had been operating since the early part of this century. City expansion had often engulfed nearby villages, thus dramatically affecting the traditional behaviour, activities and way of life of the existing inhabitants. In 1912 George Sturt ('George Bourne') described the process in detail for a village in northwest Surrey which since the turn of the century had become progressively a 'residential centre' for London. Stressing how the traditional 'peasant system' had virtually disappeared, he wrote:

> The old life is being swiftly obliterated. The valley is passing out of the hands of its former inhabitants. They are being crowded into corners, and are becoming as aliens in their own homes; they are receding before newcomers with new ideas, and, greatest change of all, they are yielding to the dominion of new ideas themselves (p. 17).
> ... The old families, continue in their old home; but they begin to be new people. (p. 117)[2]

It is this and other urbanising processes, occurring ever more widely over Britain and at an accelerating pace, which have dominated rural social change throughout this century and will continue to do so in the foreseeable future. They have resulted not only from the presence in many localities of new villagers of urban origin, but also from the various other urban influences and more intensive rural-urban interaction. But there are many indications that, from the point of view of presentday rural inhabitants as well as that of urban residents, an excessive urbanisation of the countryside, in both a physical sense and a psychosociological sense, is being considered as undesirable. Many rural people actively seek to prevent many urban traits becoming a norm in their communities. Many urban people, more openly than at any time in the past, express a value towards living in and a need to be associated with real communities, in an environment which is not congested, which appears healthy and preferably picturesque. All these conditions are imagined to exist in rural areas. It is impossible to ignore the existence of numerous nostalgic and emotive feelings in the diversity of contemporary reactions towards rural society and the countryside; at least, they indicate concern for the rural situation. But in any discussion of rural society it is important to distinguish sentimentality and imagery from reality, although taking due regard of both. The future depends not only on the continuation of many contemporary trends, but also on the actions and reactions, needs and imaginativeness of the people involved.

Future changes in British rural areas, as in the past, will depend on the interaction of internal rural forces with those operating in society at large. Local initiative, leadership and inventiveness in dealing with recognised problems and needs of the village or rural community, and enterprise on the part of individuals and groups in copying and adopting ideas from elsewhere, will be crucial. From outside, strong and possibly more intensive influences will emanate from local government and other rural agencies, as well as from national government. Increasingly, the effect of changes at the level of the individual, family and neighbourhood, and the adaptations required, imply a need for help and guidance which combine the use of valid knowledge with a full recognition of personal opinions and feelings.

Most of the work of planners employed by rural local authorities and of agricultural advisers has dealt with specific problems, present or foreseen. Despite the wide variety, the situations with which they have been concerned must as a whole be regarded as more or less normal. Social workers, on the other hand, in rural as much as in urban areas, have tended to concentrate their attention on more extreme social situations, often the problems of a specified minority, dealing usually with the individual or the family, and occasionally with a neighbourhood. There is a growing recognition of the need to combine the two approaches, where a more explicit social emphasis is introduced into local planning activity and agricultural development work. The aim must be to achieve rural development, with active assistance from various agencies whose employees help not only certain individuals or minorities in the population but the majority to recognise and understand the nature of local problems and to work actively and cooperatively towards their solution. This approach, although it may legitimately contain defensive, conservative or even preservationist elements, is in no sense negative. The aim is an equitable social betterment with positive action towards that end. This does not imply direction on the part of the professional agents of change. Rather, their necessary functions must be to spread ideas and information into communities where they might potentially be useful, and to stimulate the generation internally of creative and beneficial ideas. Their role must embrace both a sympathy and an empathy towards the rural people concerned, aiming to understand their varied aims and aspirations, to assist in their attainment, and to reconcile their diverse wishes.

Contemporary rural sociology is concerned primarily with the description and deeper understanding of change as it affects rural society, and the application of theory as well as research methods and findings to rural development.[3] In the early decades of this century, particularly in the U.S.A., this was often associated with various rural organisations, the support of a rural point of view, and an agricultural fundamentalism. By today rural sociologists are active internationally in numerous projects in developed, primarily urban nations, as well as in developing countries. In one way or another, they are broadly concerned with the improvement of rural life but usually free from any ideological position which defines rural life as essentially different from other sectors of society and as such to be highly valued.

The condition of rural life in Britain is, in general, not unlike that in many other countries, especially in Western Europe where town and city populations are now dominant and the rural society is in close and ever more intensive interaction with the urban sector. Many of the basic elements, the ongoing social processes, and the problems are broadly similar. It is one of the apparent paradoxes of such societies, where the farm population has become a small minority and continues to decline, and where the total rural population by any definition is also in the minority, that increasing attention is now being given to the rural situation and its problems. This arises not only from an urban concern for the physical environment in the countryside, but also from a general recognition that the rural society contributes in innumerable ways to the wellbeing of the total society. By means of the variety of internal social processes which are active in the countryside, and the numerous linkages with the nation as a whole, rural society demonstrates at one and the same time its differences from as well as its integration within the total society. However, many of the procedures and methods which are appropriate in an urban environment require modification, while new approaches also need to be sought, if they are to be effective among rural people.

In rather different ways, similar recognition of the significance of rural society is emerging in developing countries. Although the rapid rate of growth of urbanisation is creating their more obvious problems, to ignore the numerically dominant rural population is not only to aggravate the urban problems but to intensify existing rural problems, even to create new ones.

In all societies, rural people will continue to be present, although the nature and variety of the social elements and processes contained in rural communities, and thus their character, will change. As much as all other sectors of a society, they merit attention and understanding.

References and further reading

Most textbooks on rural sociology are of American origin. Among those published in the past fifteen years, the following provide a good coverage of the subject, although the examples and illustrations used are predominantly drawn from research studies in the U.S.A.:

Charles P. Loomis and J. Allan Beegle, *Rural Sociology: the Strategy of Change*, Prentice-Hall Inc. 1957.

A. L. Bertrand, ed., *Rural Sociology: an Analysis of Contemporary Rural Life*, McGraw-Hill, 1958.

Everett M. Rogers, *Social Change in Rural Society*, Appleton-Century-Crofts, 1960.

Walter L. Slocum, *Agricultural Sociology*, Harper, 1962.

Lee Taylor, *Urban-Rural Problems*, Belmont, Calif., Dickenson Publishing Co., 1968.

T. Lynn Smith and Paul E. Zopf jnr., *Principles of Inductive Rural Sociology*, Philadelphia, F. A. Davis, 1970.

Apart from items referred to in each chapter, attention is also drawn to the following:

F. G. Thomas, *The Changing Village. An essay on rural reconstruction*, Nelson, 1939.

Victor Bonham-Carter, *The English Village*, Penguin Books, 1952.

W. P. Baker, *The English Village*, Oxford University Press, 1953.

John Higgs, ed., *People in the Countryside: Studies in Rural Social Development*, London, National Council of Social Service, 1960.

CHAPTER 1. WHAT IS RURAL?

1. Maude F. Davies, *Life in an English village: an economic and historical survey of the parish of Corsley in Wiltshire* Fisher Unwin, 1909.
2. 'George Bourne', *Change in the Village*, Duckworth, 1912.
3. Ronald Frankenberg, *Communities in Britain, Social life in town and country*, Penguin Books, 1966.
4. Erich H. Jacoby, 'The coming backlash of semi-urbanization', *CERES* (F.A.O. Review), vol. 3, no. 6, 1970.
5. Erich H. Jacoby, *Man and Land: the fundamental issue in development*, Deutsch, 1971.
6. Population Census, *General Report on the Population Census of England and Wales, 1951*, H.M.S.O., 1958.
7. Emrys Jones, *Towns and Cities*, Oxford University Press, 1966.
8. Louis Wirth, 'Urbanism as a way of life', *American Journal of Sociology*, vol. 44, 1938.

CHAPTER 2. A CONCEPTUAL FRAMEWORK

1. Leonard Reissman, *The Urban Process*, The Free Press of Glencoe, 1964.
2. Philip M. Hauser, 'Observations on the urban-folk and urban-rural dichotomies as forms of Western ethnocentricism', in Philip M. Hauser and Leo F. Schnore, eds., *The Study of Urbanization*, Wiley, 1965, pp. 503–14 and 516–17.
3. Oscar Lewis, 'Further observations on the folk-urban continuum and urbanization, with special reference to Mexico City', in *ibid*, pp. 491–503, and 514–16.
4. R. E. Pahl, 'The rural-urban continuum', *Sociologia Ruralis*, vol. 6, pp. 299–329; reprinted pp. 263–97 in R. E. Pahl, ed., *Readings in Urban Sociology*, Pergamon Press, 1968.
5. Hauser, *op. cit.*, pp. 504 and 514.
6. Charles P. Loomis, *Social Systems: essays on their persistence and change*, Van Nostrand, 1960, p. 60.

7. Ferdinand Tonnies, *Gemeinschaft und Gesellschaft* (1887), trans. and ed. Charles Loomis (with commentary) as *Community and Society*, Michigan State University Press, 1957. Various editions are available; it is published in Britain as *Community and Association*, Routledge & Kegan Paul, 1955.

8. A. K. Constandse, Discussion on Pahl's paper in *Sociologia Ruralis*, vol. 6, 1966, pp. 375-7, reprinted in Pahl, ed., *Readings in Urban Sociology*, 1968, pp. 301-3.

9. Eugen Lupri, 'The rural-urban variable reconsidered: the cross-cultural perspective', *Sociologia Ruralis*, vol. 7, 1967, pp. 1-20.

10. R. E. Pahl, 'The rural-urban continuum: a reply to Eugen Lupri', *Sociologia Ruralis*, vol. 7, 1967, pp. 21-9.

11. Kingsley Davis, 'Conceptual analysis of stratification', *American Sociological Review*, vol. 7, 1942, pp. 309-21.

12. Loomis, *op. cit.* (ref. 7 above).

13. Aidan Southall, 'An operational theory of role', *Human Relations*, vol. 12, 1959, pp. 17-34.

14. Talcott Parsons and Edward A. Shils, eds, *Toward a General Theory of Action*, Harvard University Press, 1951, pp. 71-91.

15. Ronald Frankenberg, *Communities in Britain : social life in town and country*, Penguin Books, 1966.

16. Ronald Frankenberg 'British community studies: problems of synthesis', in Michael Banton, ed., *The Social Anthropology of Complex Societies* (A.S.A. monograph no. 4), Tavistock Publications, 1966, pp. 123-54.

17. Peter H. Mann, *An Approach to Urban Sociology*, Routledge & Kegan Paul, 1965.

18. Royal Commission on Local Government in England, *Community Attitude Survey : England* (Research Studies no. 9). H.M.S.O., 1969.

19. G. Duncan Mitchell, 'Depopulation and rural social structure', *The Sociological Review* (old series), vol. 42, 1950, section 4.

20. G. Duncan Mitchell, 'The relevance of group dynamics to rural planning problems', *The Sociological Review* (old series), vol. 43, 1951, section 1.

CHAPTER 3. RURAL WAYS OF LIFE IN BRITAIN

— 1. Joel M. Halpern, *The Changing Village Community* (Modernization of Traditional Societies Series), Prentice-Hall, 1967.
2. John Saville, 'Urbanization and the countryside', in John Higgs, ed., *People in the Countryside: studies in rural social development*. London, National Council of Social Service, 1966, p. 18.
3. Herbert Kötter, 'Changes in urban-rural relationships in industrial society', in Nels Anderson, ed., *Urbanism and Urbanization*, E. J. Brill, 1964, p. 21.
— 4. Agricultural Economics Research Institute, *Rural Planning: a study of rural problems*, Oxford University Press, 1944 (The area covered is North Oxfordshire).
— 5. M. A. Havinden, *Estate Villages: a study of the Berkshire villages of Ardington and Lockinge*, with contributions by D. S. Thornton and P. D. Wood, Lund Humphries, 1966.
6. Valerie J. Jackson, *Population in the Countryside: growth and stagnation in the Cotswolds*, Cass, 1968.
— 7. J. S. Nalson, *Mobility of Farm Families: a study of occupational and residential mobility in an upland area of England*, Manchester University Press, 1968. (Concerned with an area in the Peak District.)

Community studies

8. Alwyn D. Rees, *Life in a Welsh Countryside: a social study of Llanfihangel yng Ngwynfa*, University of Wales Press, 1950.
9. Winifred M. Whiteley, 'Littletown-in-Overspill', in Leo Kuper, ed., *Living in Towns: selected research papers in urban sociology*, Cresset Press, 1953.

10. W. M. Williams, *The Sociology of an English Village: Gosforth*, Routledge & Kegan Paul, 1956.

11. Ronald Frankenberg, *Village on the Border: a social study of religion, politics and football in a North Wales community*, Cohen and West, 1957.

12. Elwyn Davies and Alwyn D. Rees, eds, *Welsh Rural Communities*, University of Wales Press, 1960.

    This contains four studies:

    David Jenkins, 'Aberporth: a study of a coastal village in South Cardiganshire' (pp. 1–63).

    Emrys Jones, 'Tregaron: the sociology of a market town in Central Cardiganshire' (pp. 65–117).

    T. Jones Hughes, 'Aberdaron: the social geography of a small region in the Llŷn Peninsula' (pp. 119–81)

    Trefor M. Owen, 'Chapel and Community in Glan-Llyn, Merioneth' (pp. 183–248).

13. James Littlejohn, *Westrigg: the sociology of a Cheviot parish*, Routledge & Kegan Paul, 1963.

14. W. M. Williams, *A West Country Village: Ashworthy—family, kinship and land*, Routledge & Kegan Paul, 1963.

15. Isabel Emmett, *A North Wales Village: a social anthropological study*, Routledge & Kegan Paul, 1964.

16. R. E. Pahl, *Urbs in Rure: the metropolitan fringe in Hertfordshire*, London School of Economics and Political Science, Geographical Papers no. 2, 1964.

17. E. W. Martin, *The Shearers and the Shorn: a study of life in a Devon community*, Routledge & Kegan Paul, 1965.

18. Norbert Elias and John L. Scotson, *The Established and the Outsiders,* Cass, 1965.

    Other 'community studies' have been published as journal articles, or as publications from various University departments, or are contained in research theses presented at several Universities.

19. J. B. Loudon, 'Kinship and crisis in South Wales'. *British Journal of Sociology*, vol. 12, 1961, pp. 333–50.

    See also:

20. D. E. G. Plowman; W. E. Munchinton, and Margaret Stacey, 'Local social status in England and Wales', *Sociological Review* (new series), vol. 10, 1962, pp. 161–202.

CHAPTER 4. RURAL SOCIAL STRUCTURE AND ORGANISATIONS, I. FAMILY AND NEIGHBOURHOOD

1. H. Thorpe, 'Rural settlement', in J. Wreford Watson and J. B. Sissons, eds, *The British Isles : a systematic geography*, Nelson, 1964, p. 378.

2. The Scott Report, (1942) *Report of the Committee on Land Utilisation in Rural Areas* (Ministry of Planning and Works, Chairman: Sir Leslie F. Scott), H.M.S.O. 1942, Cmd 6378.

3. J. Arwel Edwards, 'The viability of lower size-order settlements in rural areas: the case of North-East England', *Sociologia Ruralis*, vol. 11, 1971, pp. 245–74.

4. See Hughes (ch. 3, ref. 12 above), pp. 158–72; and Emmett (ch. 3, ref. 15), pp. 62–8.

5. George A. Hillery, jnr, 'Definitions of community: areas of agreement', *Rural Sociology*, vol. 20, 1955, pp. 111–23.

CHAPTER 5. RURAL SOCIAL STRUCTURE AND ORGANISATION, II. THE RURAL COMMUNITY

1. Robert E. Dickinson, *City, Region and Regionalism: a geographical contribution to human ecology*, Routledge & Kegan Paul, 1947.
   (This summarises and reproduces the maps, on pages 76–92, from Dickinson's original articles on aspects of the urban geography of East Anglia, viz.
   – 'The distribution of functions of the smaller urban settlements of East Anglia,' *Geography*, vol. 17, 1932, pp. 19–31.
   – 'The markets and market areas of East Anglia', *Economic Geography*, vol. 10, 1934, pp. 172–82.

2. H. E. Bracey, *Social Provision in Rural Wiltshire*, Methuen, 1952.

3. John E. Brush and Howard E. Bracey, 'Rural service centers in Southwestern Wisconsin and Southern England', *Geographical Review*, vol. 45, 1955, pp. 559–69.

4. H. E. Bracey, 'A rural component of centrality applied to six southern counties in the United Kingdom', *Economic Geography*, vol. 32, 1956, pp. 38–50.

5. Gwyn Rowley, 'Central places in rural wales: a case study', *Tijdschrift voor Economische en Sociale Geografie*, vol. 61, 1970, pp. 32–40.

6. H. E. Bracey, *English Rural Life: village activities, organisations and institutions*, Routledge & Kegan Paul, 1959.

7. Peter Haggett, *Locational Analysis in Human Geography*, Edward Arnold, 1965.

CHAPTER 6. CHANGES IN CONTEMPORARY RURAL SOCIETY

1. See, for example, J. S. Nalson, *Mobility of Farm Families: a study of occupational and residential mobility in an upland area of England*. Manchester University Press, 1968.

2. Gwyn E. Jones, "The adoption and diffusion of agricultural practices", *World Agricultural Economics and Rural Sociology Abstracts*, vol. 9 (3), 1967, pp. 1–34.

3. Everett M. Rogers and F. Floyd Shoemaker, *Communication of Innovations: a cross cultural approach*, Free Press of Glencoe, 1971.

4. Robin Pedley, *The Comprehensive School*, Penguin Books, 1963, p. 47.

CHAPTER 7. RURAL–URBAN INTERACTION AND RURAL CHANGE

1. R. J. Green, *Country Planning: the future of the rural regions*, Manchester University Press, 1971.

2. John Saville, *Rural Depopulation in England and Wales, 1851–1951*, Routledge & Kegan Paul, 1957.

3. *Depopulation in Mid-Wales* (Welsh Office), H.M.S.O., 1964.
4. H. E. Bracey, *People and the Countryside*, Routledge & Kegan Paul, 1970.
5. *People and Planning: Report of the Committee on Public Participation in Planning* (Ministry of Housing and Local Government; Scottish Development Department; Welsh Office; Chairman: A. M. Skeffington) H.M.S.O., 1969.
6. David C. Thorns, 'Participation in rural planning', *International Review of Community Development*, No. 23–24, 1970, pp. 129–37.
7. *Settlement in the Countryside: a planning method*, (Ministry of Housing and Local Government; Welsh Office), H.M.S.O., 1967, p. 7, para. 31.
8. Peter Self and Herbert J. Storing, *The State and the Farmer*, Allen & Unwin, 1962.

CHAPTER 8. FUTURE PROSPECTS

1. C. S. Orwin, *Problems of the Countryside*, Cambridge University Press, 1945.
2. 'George Bourne', *Change in the Village*, Duckworth, 1912.
3. A. K. Constandse and E. W. Hofstee, *Rural Sociology in Action*, (F.A.O. Agricultural Development Paper, no. 79), Rome (Food and Agricultural Organization of the United Nations), 1964.

Index